From Victim to Victor: Breaking the Chains of Narcissistic Abuse

Unmasking Emotional Manipulation, Rebuilding Self-Worth, and Cultivating Unshakable Resilience

Melanie Catlin Schaafsma, MSW, PhD

Table of Contents

Trigger warning: This book covers sensitive themes related to abuse that some readers may find distressing.

Introduction

*Toxic people attach themselves like cinder blocks to your ankles and then invite you for a swim in their poisoned waters. –*John Mark Green

Katherine sits on the couch retelling horrific experiences from her childhood. She narrates one specific incident from when she was six years old and had tried to make a beautiful breakfast spread for her mother on Mother's Day. She recalls how she'd enlisted her father's help to prepare the toast and cut her mother's favorite fruit. Then she stood on a chair to reach for the peanut butter and jelly and messily spread them onto the toast, before going to the small flower bed outside the front door to pick her mother's favorite morning glories to decorate the breakfast tray.

Though she'd pestered her father to help, he'd actually only made the toast, then left for the office with a, "Try not to upset your mother today, at least." But nothing could dampen Katherine's excitement. She went into her mother's bedroom with a precariously balanced tray, placed it next to the bed, and jumped into bed with her mother to wake her up.

However, all her excitement vanished the moment she saw the expression on her mother's face.

"What on earth do you think you're doing?! How many times have I told you not to come into this bedroom without knocking!" her mother chided her.

"But I was trying to surprise you, Mommy! Happy Mother's Day! Look what I made!" Katherine said proudly, pointing to the messy breakfast tray.

"Katherine, I hope my kitchen isn't as messy as this plate. How am I supposed to eat this soggy toast? And why would you put all these leaves and flowers on food? Do you expect me to eat this?!"

Katherine then goes on to describe how her mother went on a rant about how she, Katherine, had only made her life more difficult. She even gave her a time-out for all the mess she'd created in the kitchen.

This is only one of the incidents that Katherine describes throughout multiple therapy sessions. What's intriguing is that even though the cruelty of her mother's words and actions are obvious to any objective observer, Katherine still struggles to accept this unkind upbringing. It's almost as if talking about it would make her sound ungrateful or even unjustifiably entitled. *After all, love and kindness must be earned.*

Even as Katherine undergoes therapy, she still struggles to accept that she was emotionally abused. Whenever I gently confront her with this possibility, she responds with disclaimers such as, "Don't get me wrong; I had a great childhood. My parents never laid a hand on me. They're very nice people. And I had all the comforts that anyone could ask for. I suppose every family has its issues, doesn't it?"

Recognizing the Abuse Is the First Step

Abuse is a triggering word for many of us, yet not everyone understands it fully. This lack of understanding is largely responsible for our inability to recognize the signs of abuse as they manifest in our own lives. The moment I say abuse, your mind may jump straight to violence—physical or sexual. However, this one-dimensional view of abuse often keeps us from understanding the big-picture perpetration of abusive dynamics.

When assessing abuse in any relationship, it's important to note that physical or even sexual abuse doesn't just happen out of the blue. Rather, it's much more likely that the physical or sexual act is a culmination of abusive patterns that have been present for years. This is especially true in the case of romantic partners. Reports suggest that

95% of perpetrators who abuse their partners physically also abuse them emotionally (Domestic Violence Center of Chester County, n.d.). This is why an understanding of abuse beyond outward actions is essential.

Unfortunately, Katherine isn't the only one who struggles with identifying emotional abuse in her life. In my years as a therapist, I've come across several clients who have an almost black-and-white notion of what abuse looks like. For instance, they vehemently oppose the idea of one person using physical force against another. However, this sense of conviction seems to go missing the moment physical force is replaced by cruel, traumatizing words. What people may not realize is that psychological abuse can scar a person's psyche just as badly as physical abuse. Without understanding the subtleties of abuse in its emotional and psychological form, it's impossible to heal.

Are You Suffering From Emotional Abuse?

Theoretically, emotional abuse is easy to understand—it can be defined as any behavior intended to threaten, isolate, control, or manipulate you. While the aggression associated with physical abuse makes it easier to identify, the same cannot be said for emotional abuse. For all you know, your (emotional) abuser may be a sweet-talking, charming, seemingly funny and witty loved one who keeps you trapped in a web of manipulations without you even being aware of it.

This, I've found, is the primary reason why victims of emotional abuse find it hard to come to terms with the fact they're being abused. It's almost as if they themselves, or their overall ecosystem at large, have conditioned them to believe these abusive patterns are simply an expression of care and affection.

Take Katherine's case, for example. It took her quite a while to even make peace with the fact that she didn't deserve her mother's constant condescension and contempt. This was mainly because the scorn and disdain were often thinly veiled as a concerned parent's bid to get her to somehow improve. Katherine frequently said in our sessions that she always felt that if only she could be "just a tad better," she'd gain her mother's approval. Unfortunately, however, her mother always pushed that coveted approval just a little farther out of reach, no matter how hard Katherine tried. This infinite pursuit left her flailing in a sea of overwhelming emotions of anxiety, shame, guilt, anger, helplessness, and sometimes just plain confusion about what she'd done wrong.

As much as I'd like to say otherwise, this is the gut-wrenching experience most emotional abuse victims go through on a daily basis. We'll explore various dimensions of many such experiences throughout this book. But before going further, I urge you to take the following test to gain clarity about your personal experience with emotional abuse.

Think of toxic exchanges with one specific person—it may be a romantic partner, a parent, a sibling, a friend, or someone you share a professional relationship with. While ups and downs are perfectly natural in any relationship, here, you want to pay attention to the frequency and intensity of these toxic interactions and their impact on your well-being. Remember that this isn't a standardized questionnaire. Therefore, it mustn't be used for scoring purposes but is instead intended to facilitate insightful introspection. Keep your responses in mind as you go through this book as they'll help you make sense of your own experience.

Respond to the following questions with "never," "rarely," "sometimes," "often," or "always":

1. They belittle my thoughts, and opinions without any regard for my feelings.

2. I find myself walking on eggshells around them, hoping not to upset them in any way.

3. They tend to intimidate me into doing things I may not wish to do or feel uncomfortable doing.

4. They use emotional blackmail to get their way.

5. They stop me from being around my friends and family.

6. They put words in my mouth or completely twist what I say to prove their point.

7. Their sarcasm and ridicule make me feel unsure of myself.

8. Withholding affection and using the silent treatment is their go-to way of getting me to do things.

9. They restrict my financial access every time we fight.

10. They find a way to blame me for their out-of-control behaviors.

The Politics of Gender and Abuse

According to the Centers for Disease Control and Prevention, one in four women and one in seven men will experience physical violence by their intimate partner at some point during their lifetime (Huecker et al., 2023). The gender differences in the reporting of physical abuse in intimate relationships may seem deceptively clear, but the reality may point to something else.

Note that reported figures can be widely different from actual experiences. It's often seen that men are not nearly as likely to report physical abuse by a woman because of shame resulting from their "manly conditioning." Unless a serious enough injury lands them in the hospital or the police become involved, many men never report physical abuse by their female intimate partners.

These lines become much more blurry when it comes to emotional abuse. Data suggests that an almost equal percentage of men and women (48.8% and 48.4%, respectively) are emotionally abused by their partners (Domestic Violence Center of Chester County, n.d.). On the other hand, according to one study, 86% of women reported being emotionally abusive in their relationships compared to 82% of men (Karakurt & Silver, 2013). Now, the purpose isn't to get lost in the storm of statistics but rather to understand that victims of psychological abuse may belong to any gender—and no individual's experience can be trivialized.

That being said, we also must be sensitive to how certain marginalized populations may be more vulnerable to this kind of abuse. Take, for instance, children or women, who may be financially dependent on their abusive partners. These partners may not necessarily be men, but the skewed power dynamics make it particularly easy for the abuser to cut off their victims from any kind of social support.

In this book, we'll explore all kinds of abuse regardless of the gender of the abuser and the victim. However, wherever appropriate, we may also discuss power dynamics entangled with gender role expectations as they contribute to abuse.

Debunking Some Myths Before We Get Started

Even though emotional abuse is something many people struggle with in their daily lives, it's still greatly shrouded in mystery. The topic of abuse itself is so taboo that even talking about it is unthinkable for most. However, to truly grasp how emotional abuse impacts your life, you must re-evaluate the way in which you perceive this experience. We've already burst one of the most common myths: that women are always the abused and men the abusers. Let's debunk a few more common misconceptions before we begin:

- **Some responsibility for the abuse always lies with the victim:** It's not uncommon for abuse victims to internalize the abuse, which leads them to think they deserve it all. The victims may even go on to develop a critical self-talk that mimics their abusers: *I shouldn't have upset them. I should have set better boundaries. I put myself in that situation.* It must be highlighted that no victim *deserves* to be abused. The full responsibility for abuse undeniably lies with the abuser. Period.

- **Only certain types of people get abused:** While it would be convenient to think of abuse as only affecting meek personalities, the reality is very different. Remember that abuse is more a function of the abuser's personality traits than those of the abused. We'll talk more about these personality traits in coming chapters.

- **There's no such thing as emotional abuse—some people just express their care differently:** As mentioned earlier, abuse often disguises itself as love and concern. How often have you heard the phrase "tough love"? Quite often, I'll bet! This idea of tough love can make it extremely hard to recognize verbal and psychological abuse. After all, how can you blame a loved one who only wishes the best for you? But the truth is, this kind of abuse ends up doing a lot more harm when it comes from a loved one.

- **Emotional abuse isn't as serious as physical or sexual abuse:** People often think of emotional and verbal abuse as new-age concepts that hold no real meaning. These are the same people who wouldn't consider a behavior abusive unless and until it causes some physical harm. The truth is, abuse in any form is equally damaging. While physical wounds heal, the havoc that abuse wreaks on a person's emotional well-being may fester under the surface, completely unknown to them.

- **The abuser doesn't mean any harm; they just have a bad temper:** The last issue that can be an obstacle in our understanding of abuse is the concessions we make to accommodate the abuser's actions. The abuser is often portrayed as someone who has no control over their words and actions when they get mad. All this does is shift the responsibility for abuse from the abuser to the abused: "When you know someone has a bad temper, why would you invite trouble by provoking them?" As you can see, this myth goes hand in hand with our first myth and can turn into just another version of victim-blaming.

A gentle reminder: Your belief in these myths may not disappear overnight, thanks to the conditioning we've all been subjected to. However, it's still crucial that you remind yourself to dispute these myths whenever they seem to take over.

Making the Most of This Book

The book is divided into two parts.

Part I: Understanding Abuse

Here, the chapters explore abuse from several vantage points—conceptual, social, personal, relationships, and so on. This is essential because our ideas about abuse can change from one setting to another. For instance, it may be easy to recognize derogatory, sarcastic remarks as abuse in an office setting, but similar remarks from a romantic partner may be dismissed as a joke. Both hurt your mental health. Therefore, recognizing abuse for what it is may require you to assess your existing beliefs. The chapters in Part I will equip you with assessments and practical tips to make this journey a little easier.

Part II: Healing Yourself

Part II is all about strategies you can use to leave behind the toxicity you've recognized. People who are blissfully unaware of what abuse can do to a person often ask me this: "Why would anyone stay in an abusive relationship? Why wouldn't they just leave?" Well, the reasons are infinite, but one of the most common is the comfort zone. Humans are wired to pick the known over the unknown. Even when the known life may be chipping away at who you are, the discomfort of an uncertain future may keep you nailed to your current life. The strategies discussed here will help you take that first step toward a new life.

This book tackles several sensitive themes. While I encourage you to persevere through the mental blocks you may encounter as you go through them, I also urge you to prioritize your well-being. If at any point you feel overwhelmed or unable to continue, be sure to seek appropriate professional help. Going on this journey will not be the easiest thing to do, but I assure you the view is much more fulfilling from the other side. This is the hero's adventure that your soul has been waiting for—when you feel ready, let's take the leap.

Part I: Understanding Abuse

Chapter 1:

The Psychology of Abuse

One word that frequently pops up in the context of emotional abuse is narcissism. The word itself comes from a Greek mythical character known as Narcissus, and nothing describes a narcissistic personality like the well-known myth (History Today, 2018).

Narcissus was the son of the river god Cephissus and the nymph Liriope. He was known far and wide for his beauty, which gained him many admirers. It was professed that he would live a long life—provided he never looked at himself. He rejected several suitors, one of whom was Echo. She was so hurt by his rejection that she completely withdrew from the world, and all that was left of her was a whisper.

The goddess Nemesis was touched by this tragedy and wanted to avenge Echo's passing. She cursed Narcissus to fall in love with his own reflection. One day when he was walking past a lake in the woods, he saw his own reflection and was so enamored by it that he refused to leave. He perished while staring at himself and seeing nothing else but his own beauty.

This exaggerated and obsessive self-love is a common pattern among all emotional abusers. Don't get me wrong; self-love is a great thing. However, exploiting those around you in pursuit of that self-love is a classic narcissistic trait. If you've ever wondered why an abuser goes to such great lengths to control their victim, understanding this *delusion of self-love* might give you some answers. This chapter will give you an insight into the possible agendas behind an abuser's behavior.

Inside the Mind of a Narcissistic Abuser

If you've ever interacted with a narcissist, you've undoubtedly witnessed someone who thinks the universe revolves around them. This trait can be annoying at best and emotionally damaging in its worst form. Be that as it may, the goal here isn't to vilify narcissistic personality disorder as a condition. Our sole focus is the narcissistic abuse that ensues as a result of this condition.

One core element of decoding this narcissistic abuse is understanding the delusion of self-love that I mentioned above. Even though it may seem like it, a narcissist doesn't love themself; rather, they love the version of themself that you reflect back to them. Too complicated? Let me explain. When you react to a narcissist's deeply hurtful comments, you mirror back to them a superior version of themself— and the power that comes with that version is exactly what they love. Please note that I'm only trying to explain the dynamics of the interaction here, not indicating that you should take responsibility for the narcissist's delusion of self-love.

While it's tempting to view all narcissistic abusers through the same lens, they may actually belong to different categories. Generally, narcissists are one of five types (Dorwart, 2024):

- **Overt:** These are what some would call the classic narcissists. They're the ones who loudly show off their new car at a funeral. They display no empathy for others. It's almost as if they're starring in a movie in their own mind where they're the ultimate lead, with others as their entourage in the background. They can go to extreme lengths to fulfill their own desires, with no regard for how their actions may impact others. Think of a bully who traumatizes the weaker kids in class to project an image of strength and confidence.

- What's interesting is that though overt narcissists really crave validation and attention, they totally fail to give it to others. On the other hand, the criticism they dish out so generously gravely threatens them when they receive it from others. Flying into a narcissistic rage the moment someone gives them any negative feedback is an excellent example of someone who feels deeply threatened.

- **Covert:** While overt narcissistic abusers are easy to spot, covert narcissists may not be. Also known as closet narcissists, these abusers often use passive tactics rather than direct aggression to fulfill their ulterior motives. Think of the mean girl clique in classic Hollywood chick flicks. They aren't the same as the bullies who use force. Much to the contrary, they project an image of popularity—and maybe even kindness. Yet their passive-aggressive methods end up causing substantial turmoil in others' lives.

- These analogies may paint a picture of school-related abuse, but beware—these passive-aggressive bullies may indulge in their abusive patterns well beyond their school years. You'll find them frequently engaging in shaming, manipulation, guilt-tripping, blaming, or even giving the silent treatment to get their way. That last one is a special favorite for many. Remember that Beatles song "I'm Looking Through You"? Check it out if you don't know it and you'll see how damaging ignoring someone can be. This kind of abuse strips a person of their basic dignity—it can make them feel like they aren't even worth paying attention to. Such treatment, especially at the hands of a loved one whose opinion you value, can have massive negative effects in the long run.

- **Antagonistic:** While all narcissistic abusers are deeply concerned about their "better than the rest" image, this type of narcissist is particularly focused on being perceived as the best. Now, this mustn't be confused with being ambitious; they don't necessarily have high goals, but are more interested in besting others in their interactions. For instance, in an argument, an antagonistic narcissist is likely to bring up your past errors or personal flaws to discredit you rather than bring up valid, verifiable facts. They often derive great pleasure from making you feel inferior. This twisted sense of competitiveness means they're likely to hold grudges about something you don't even remember and use it to belittle you when you least expect it.

- Antagonistic abusers seem to have a distinct, almost desperate need for attention and compliance. The moment they feel this need isn't being fulfilled as per their expectations, they tend to lash out with threats, criticism, manipulation, exploitation, and even physical violence. Relationships with these abusers can be particularly draining because they make you believe you're everything that's wrong with the relationship.

- **Communal:** This one's a bit tricky—while all other kinds of narcissists prefer to ride the high of putting others down, communal narcissists may actually be doing some good for their community. They participate proactively in charitable causes and seem to have a high sense of altruism. Where's the problem with that? Well, the problem lies in the fact that they're doing all these things for social validation rather than the cause itself. So, a communal narcissist may buy a meal for a homeless person, but they're more interested in posing for social media pictures and posts during this good deed than the deed itself. You may argue that we all do things for external praise at some point. Sure, receiving appreciation in the form of a "thank you" feels wonderful, but for most healthy people, it isn't the prime motivation for helping someone.

- Not only do communal narcissists love the praise and attention that their so-called good deeds bring them, but they also love to throw their holier-than-thou attitudes in others' faces. These individuals will love telling you about how they sacrificed going to a party to attend a charitable event and will then belittle you for not doing the same. Moreover, not receiving the validation they expect can make them lash out with irritability and ridicule, especially toward the people closest to them. Abuse from communal narcissists can be especially tricky, because this vengeful dark side that their loved ones see just doesn't align with their public image as a saintly model citizen. This can make it particularly difficult for the victims to gain the required support as people might tell them they, rather than the hidden abuser, are the problem.

- **Malignant:** Dr. Ramani Durvasula, an American clinical psychologist and an expert on everything related to narcissism, refers to this form of narcissism as "the last stop on the train before it turns the direction towards psychopathy" (DoctorRamani, 2020c). Now, the moment you hear psychopathy, your mind may jump to a psychopathic killer, thanks to all those creepy Hollywood movies! But hold your horses just a moment—not all psychopaths are killers. Psychopathy in its most basic form can be thought of as a willful disregard for the safety and well-being of others. Psychopaths tend to be so focused on their own needs, desires, and pleasures that they don't mind endangering someone else for those purposes. They may have a cold, apathetic, self-centric, and even antisocial outlook that strongly indicates a total lack of conscience.

- Malignant narcissists share many of these psychopathic traits and may exhibit patterns such as exploitativeness, coercive control, and menacing cruelty in their interactions. The intensity and frequency of these patterns tend to be much lower in other forms of narcissism. The irony is that malignant narcissists deceive people regularly without any remorse, yet are almost paranoid about people deceiving them. For instance, while they may frequently lie to their partner to serve their own purposes, they may also wrongfully accuse them of cheating. This sense of victimization is accompanied by fits of rage, characterized by screaming, cursing, hurling objects, or even aggression toward people.

- These fits of rage and loss of emotional control might be the one factor that distinguishes them from psychopaths as described in psychological literature. While malignant narcissists are prone to noisy reactive outbursts with lots of yelling and crying, psychopaths can stay calm even when angry (Durvasula, 2024). They do display dramatic emotions when it suits them, but those emotions don't result from hurt feelings or insecurity but rather from a calculated choice to exploit others.

If you look up types of narcissism online, you may find a few more types and labels too. Here, I've tried to focus on the five categories of narcissism that are most relevant to emotional abuse. Victims of this narcissistic emotional abuse often wonder how they came to have any relationship at all with their abusers, given their toxic traits. This is one of the ways in which victims of emotional abuse blame themselves, thinking: *There must be something wrong with me if I attract such people in my life!* If your mind has ever gone on this flawed track, I'm here to tell you that things aren't that simple.

The Disastrous Pull Between Narcissists and Empaths

You'll often hear that narcissists lack the capacity to be empathic and that they simply don't care about other people's feelings. While the second part of this statement may well be true, the first part isn't all that simple. To understand this, let's first try to understand what empathy really means.

Empathy can be defined as an individual's ability to feel others' emotions as if you were experiencing them yourself. This requires that you place yourself in another person's shoes and imagine the situation from their perspective. There are two critical aspects here: One is retaining an intact awareness of the boundary between your emotions and those of others, while the second is having the ability to understand their worldview. So, essentially, two components can be identified here: affective/emotional and cognitive.

For a long time, it was believed that both of these aspects of empathy were hampered in narcissistic individuals (Jonason & Krause, 2013). However, newer research suggests that though narcissists aren't particularly great at the affective component, their capacity for cognitive empathy is quite alright (Turner et al., 2019). In other words, narcissists often know what you're going through but just don't feel it on an emotional level.

This means they tend to have a pretty accurate understanding of what their victims feel as a result of their actions. This may not be true of all narcissists, but those who possess this awareness are called empathic narcissists. Rather than using their emotional understanding to better the situation, these empathic narcissists often weaponize empathy in a way that emotionally destroys their victims.

Many narcissistic abusers put up an elaborate illusion of self-victimization even though they're the real perpetrator. In their twisted version of reality, they often portray themselves as either the troubled victim or the all-overcoming hero, while painting their victims as the ultimate villains. The narcissist will use their skill of cognitive empathy to nudge their victims to share their darkest secrets, fears, apprehensions, and anxieties, then use those vulnerabilities to manufacture a reality in which they're being abused at the hands of their victims. This triggers a seemingly unending cycle of emotional blackmail, guilt-tripping, and passive-aggressive control.

Now, considering the intense role that empathy and emotions play in this dynamic, it's not surprising that narcissistic abusers oftentimes find convenient targets in empaths. An empath is any individual who's deeply attuned to their own and others' emotions. They're wonderfully mindful of the triggers and sensitivities that they themselves or others may have, and they try their best to create an environment of support and encouragement. They tend to forgive easily, thanks to their trusting nature, and never seem to reach their limit of giving other people second chances. However, these overly empathetic patterns also tend to fuel the narcissistic delusion.

Narcissistic abusers have a way of appealing to this trusting and forgiving side of empaths. These empath/narcissist encounters can turn quite problematic, as the narcissist keeps weaving an infinite web of grandiosity while the empath unknowingly keeps validating the lies. As the relationship deepens, the empath may realize the draining nature of their encounters. However, their persistence in "making the relationship work" only digs them deeper and deeper into a hole of self-doubt. By the time they realize they need to get out, the narcissist already has an elaborate tool kit to keep them trapped. It's almost as if the narcissists latch on to these forgiving caregivers with all their might (until their next target comes along) and slowly sap them of their life energy.

I know it sounds as if narcissists are all around you, laying their traps and getting ready to hunt their prey. But the truth is, that's exactly what a narcissistic abuser does to keep their victim locked in. It's worth taking a look at the cycle of abuse that ensues.

The Never-Ending Cycle of Abuse

Narcissistic abuse seems to follow a very particular pattern. According to the clinical psychologist Dr. Aimee Daramus, it tends to progress in four main stages (Gupta, 2024):

1. **Idealizing:** In this stage, a narcissistic abuser will absolutely disarm you with their charm and confidence. In the context of a romantic relationship, the narcissist will make you feel like they have eyes and ears for no one other than you. They'll make you feel special with something known as "love-bombing," which is bombarding you with gifts, kind gestures, and sweeping compliments. They'll make you believe they're head over heels in love with you and create a serendipitous sense of destiny bringing you together. They'll show interest in getting to know everything about you, big and small, and they'll put you on a pedestal like no one else.

   If this feels a tad too much as you read, that's exactly what it feels like in a relationship, too. However, you may ignore your apprehensions because the abuser seems so persuasive and caring, thinking, *After all, it's part of the wooing stage, isn't it?* Mind you, even during this stage, there may be subtle red flags popping up in terms of control tactics or confusing messaging. The narcissist may lovingly scold you for wearing certain clothes or hanging out with your friends instead of spending time with them. Someone who has no clue of what's to come may label these instances silly or even adorable. It's only when the novelty fades that you may be forced to take off the rose-colored glasses.

   Here are a few things that a narcissistic abuser might say during this first stage:

   "I've never met someone as beautiful/understanding/loving as you."

   "We have a cosmic connection—we were just meant to be."

"You're the only one who understands me."

I'd do anything to prove my love for you."

"I'm so lucky to have found the perfect soulmate."

2. **Devaluing:** Then comes the second stage, where the narcissist will start pushing you off the pedestal just as randomly as they put you on it. This stage, however, unfolds much more slowly than the first—almost as if you're peeling the layers of an onion, each bringing more tears. The problem is, the abuser doesn't do this in an obvious manner; instead, they drop passive-aggressive clues that the victim is expected to decipher. Think of this as an exhausting and frustrating treasure hunt where the "treasure" that awaits you is just more of the ongoing toxicity.

This stage is full of chaos and confusion for the victim. They're left genuinely wondering what they've done to be on the receiving end of numerous negative exchanges such as backhanded compliments, the sudden withdrawal of validation, repetitive criticism, frequent silent treatments, and sarcastic "jokes" that are hurtful rather than funny. The person who used to worship them has suddenly turned into a harsh, almost destructive critic.

For instance, it may be something as minor as a wife forgetting to ask how her husband's morning workout was. The narcissistic husband will hold a grudge for days about not getting the attention he thinks he deserves. He may proceed to make unfair comparisons with others' spouses and how caring and wonderful they are. He may even sprinkle a dash of self-victimization on top by telling his wife how he feels like a complete fool for thinking she was so caring in the beginning. He may completely overlook the fact that he walked straight into the shower and then left for the office and his wife had no chance to strike up a conversation. The wife then starts wondering if she is really that inconsiderate and goes to great lengths to make it up to her husband, which only fuels his narcissistic tendencies.

Here are a few statements you might start hearing at this stage; note how starkly these contradict the ones from the first stage:

"Why are you acting crazy?"

"You never cared for me! I can't believe how selfish you are."

"Why do you always have to be so dramatic and sensitive?"

"If you're like this with me, I can't imagine what you're like with others. No wonder you have no real friends."

"No one can put up with all your drama but me."

3. **Repeating:** The second stage can leave you feeling drained and depressed. By now, the accusatory outbursts are a common occurrence and you've learned to walk on eggshells so as not to upset the narcissist. The first two stages have become repetitive by now—after every episode of devaluing, there's a period where the narcissist may idealize you again, thereby giving you hope that the relationship can improve. But, alas, you soon find yourself in the same emotionally burdened phase yet again—and the cycle continues.

    A common pattern observed here is that the narcissist seems to move from devaluing back to idealizing with no explanation at all. So, they may have an extremely exploitative emotional outburst one day and then move on the next day as if nothing happened. This only worsens the chaos in the victim's psyche because, no matter how hard they try, they just cannot seem to control or even predict the outcome.

4. **Discarding:** This final stage is when the relationship ends. It may be the abuser's choice, as they decide that the victim no longer serves the purpose they were intended to serve, or the victim may decide to walk out because they can't take it

anymore. While the abuser moves on quite swiftly in the first scenario, the second case almost always gets messy. The abuser will likely pursue the victim, love-bombing them to win them back; unfortunately, many victims get sucked right back in. Needless to say, the above cycle keeps going on a loop until the abuser gets bored or the victim decides to put a stop to it.

In this stage, the narcissist might tell you things like this:

"Enjoy being lonely and miserable after we break up."

"You'll never have anyone as good as me. You never deserved me to begin with."

"I've warned you over and over and yet you never paid any attention. Now look what you're making me do!"

"You're the worst partner/employee/friend/child ever. I don't know what I did to deserve the punishment of being with you all this while."

"You're the worst mistake I ever made. My life is going to be so much better without you in it."

When you pay attention to this cycle, you'll notice that these stages are accompanied by a sense of impending doom while the tension builds, followed by an abusive episode, which in turn is followed by reconciliation attempts with grand gestures, then a period of calm and quiet before the tension starts building again. Whenever I educate my clients about this cycle of abuse, they express extreme relief about finally bringing some order to the chaos. It's almost revelatory to them that they had nothing to do with the volatility their abuser exhibited all along.

Avoiding the Jaded Encounters

One thing I repeatedly remind my clients of is not to blame themselves for the abuse. Though this is obvious to a bystander, the victim doesn't always see themself as blameless. They frequently get caught in a different pattern that's harmful in a whole new way—the JADE pattern, which is an acronym for justifying, arguing, defending, and explaining:

- **Justifying:** Sustaining a satisfying relationship with a narcissistic abuser is impossible. Victims of these interactions repeatedly find themselves trying to justify their actions to their abusers. They hope that somehow they'll convince them of their loyalty and commitment to the relationship, but it never really works.

- **Arguing:** While regular arguments are a part of any healthy relationship, any disagreements with a narcissistic abuser can easily escalate into name-calling, blame-shifting, yelling, and so on. With the abuser constantly hurling ridicule at you, these unhealthy arguments can be particularly hard to escape. Yet it's important to remind yourself that this kind of arguing does no good for your own mental health.

- **Defending:** When the narcissist comes at you with the worst possible accusations and derogatory remarks, it's only natural to get defensive. Remember, however, that even though it may seem like you're standing up for yourself, your defensiveness is only sucking you deeper into your dysfunctional bond with the narcissistic abuser.

- **Explaining:** Many victims of narcissistic abuse have so completely submitted to their abuser's control that they feel they have to explain every action to their abuser to avoid upsetting them. The hope is that if they take the narcissist into their confidence and be completely honest with them, their relationship might just take a turn for the better. Unfortunately, this never happens, and the explanations only give the abuser more ammunition to use in their next attack.

When dealing with narcissists, it's best to avoid falling into the JADE trap. The most effective strategy is to cut yourself off from them, but if that's not possible, responding with short responses such as "I don't agree with that" or "I'll think about it," then walking away, also works. We'll talk more about this a little later. For now, suffice it to say that nothing makes a narcissistic abuser more mad than people who don't engage.

Your Checklist to Identify Abuse

While these patterns are much easier to see in retrospect, they might be challenging to gauge as they unfold in the moment. This is why it may be helpful to keep a checklist that you can go back to when you feel overwhelmed. We've already discussed love-bombing and the "walking on eggshells" syndrome, which are both very telling signs of incoming abuse. Let's look at a few more that may help you spot a narcissistic abuser:

- **Gaslighting:** This term comes from a 1938 British play called *Gas Light* in which the husband manipulates his wife into doubting her own memory and perceptions by dimming the intensity of the gas lights when she's alone at home (Merriam-Webster, n.d.). The wife ultimately starts questioning her own sanity and becomes completely dependent on her husband, whose plan is to have her committed to an insane asylum so he can take over her fortune. This perfectly, albeit a little simplistically, describes this common tactic used by narcissistic abusers. The abuser might tell you something then, when you talk about it later, may deny having said anything at all. They may even look you in the eyes and say something like, "You must be dreaming! Where did you ever get such an idea?" They make their victims question their reality so frequently that the victim completely drowns in self-doubt.

- **Emotional blackmail:** Narcissists love to engage in emotional blackmail, where they use sensitive information you may have shared with them in confidence to weaken your self-esteem and further deepen your dependency on them.

- **Overstepping boundaries:** Narcissistic abusers think so highly of themselves that they may believe they have the right to disregard any boundaries you've set for them. Any retaliation from your side would likely be met with more accusations, outbursts, and blackmail.

- **Projection:** This is a common narcissistic pattern in which the narcissist refuses to take any responsibility and often projects negative behaviors and the consequent blame onto you. For instance, they may accuse you of hating them, then blame you for not making any effort in the relationship—when, in reality, they're the ones who wish to make no effort.

- **Unrelenting criticism:** Constructive criticism is undoubtedly something that helps you grow. However, criticism by a narcissist is anything but constructive. They're great at making you feel like you can do nothing right. Moreover, the object of criticism isn't limited to your behaviors but may become very personal, such as your height, your weight, and even the sound of your voice. If that's not enough to get you down, they also know how to wield their criticism at the most opportune time. They'll wait until there's a group of people around whom you really like, then find the perfect moment to make fun of you or bring up your failures or secrets (jokingly, of course). This is often in retaliation to you trying to stand up for yourself at home, attempting to set boundaries with them, or telling them they're being unfair.

As helpful as this broad understanding of emotional abuse is, it's critical that you're also aware of the specific tactics that an abusive narcissist uses to keep their victims under their thumb. We'll cover these tactics in the next chapter.

Chapter 2:

The Abuser's Playbook

Have you ever wondered what it would be like to fill a bottomless pit with something? I can almost hear you exclaiming, "That's ridiculous! Why would anyone try if the pit is bottomless?" You're absolutely right: It's pointless, to say the least, yet you'll find yourself doing something similar in your interactions with an emotional abuser. Trying to please an abuser is a thankless but full-time job—no matter how hard you try, you'll never be paid in the currency of appreciation.

There's an intriguing concept in narcissistic abuse known as the "narcissistic supply." This is nothing but the narcissist's desperate, pathological need for attention, validation, and praise. The term "supply" almost perfectly describes the transactional nature of social interactions for a narcissist—for them, you're only as good as the admiration you give them. The moment this worship is soured by even minor criticism, you may be either brutally discarded altogether or coerced into worshipping them again.

This coercion can take on multiple forms. In the previous chapter, we discussed broad manipulation tactics such as love-bombing, gaslighting, and the silent treatment. This chapter will help you uncover the specific insidious strategies that an abuser may use on you.

An Inventory of the Manipulator's Methods

If you're in the first stage of the abuse cycle discussed in the previous chapter, it may be inconceivable to think that a person who seems so caring in the beginning can change so drastically. However, what you need to remember is that abuse may not always be obvious right from the get-go. Oftentimes, the abuse is lurking in the shadows disguised as sarcasm. Of course, this won't be obvious to the unsuspecting eye, but once you know what to look for, the signs become loud and clear. Take a look at the following patterns that scream "narcissist" anytime they come up in your relationship.

Triangulation

Triangulation is all about involving a third person in a relationship to influence the very core dynamics of that relationship. While the other two people are pitted against each other, the abuser gets to sit back, watch the show, and ultimately play God by resolving the chaos they themself created. This can happen in several different scenarios but is most commonly seen in families with children. While triangulation and the resulting emotional abuse occur more commonly in families with multiple children, it can also occur in families with an only child. Let's try to understand these cases before moving on to other contexts.

Have you noticed how in most families there's one "golden child" while the rest aren't given the same special treatment? Sure, in many settings this may be looked at as nothing more than a joke, but in other cases this distinction can turn quite menacing. Here, the abuser may treat children differently with the aim of creating discord between them. While the two siblings end up viewing each other negatively, they often have quite a close relationship with the abuser. This closeness affords the abuser the unique advantage of being able to twist each party's words against the other and fuel the conflict even further. As the conflict worsens, the abuser will frequently emerge as the savior, making it appear as if they're trying to resolve the problem when, in reality, they only worsen the chaos.

In families with an only child, the triangulation dynamic is slightly different. Here, the child often gets pulled into parental conflict and is manipulated into siding with one parent over the other. In these cases, one parent may complain about the other to the child, putting them in an awkward spot. Take, for instance, a mother who whines about how the father is a lazy freeloader who does nothing but make her life difficult. When a child becomes the confidant of one of their parents, they may grow up with an ever-looming anxiety because they're never really sure when things will go from bad to worse. They may frequently turn to lying to manipulate their rival parents for their own gain. However, it's not all fun and games: They also may have to bear the heavy burden of distracting their parents or being their messengers to minimize conflict. On top of everything, they also may start believing they're somehow the cause of their parents' worsening relationship.

While children are among the most vulnerable and unassuming victims of triangulation, it can be used against adults, too. A potent means of doing so is making repeated comparisons with others. For instance, an abusive partner may slide something like, "My colleague does a full-time job, takes care of their children, and still manages to look awesome! I don't have to tell you that not everyone can manage that" into the conversation in a very casual manner. On the surface, this may not feel like a particularly harmful comment, but these remarks are repeated to the point that the victims start feeling "less than," as if they're doing something wrong. And you know the most interesting part? Often, the victim may begin to harbor negative feelings against the random person they're being compared to rather than the abuser who's sowing the seeds of comparison. Remember that this can happen in any kind of setting—personal or professional—but often has the same debilitating effects on the victim's mental well-being.

Projection

We discussed projection in the previous chapter, but there's a lot more to it than a simple one-line definition. Let's try to understand this complex strategy.

The concept of projection originally came from the psychoanalytic theory that proposes projection as an unconscious defense mechanism in which a person attributes their own unacceptable feelings and desires to someone else (Vinney, 2024). However, when used in the context of narcissism, this attribution is rarely ever unconscious, per se. Projection is the narcissist's way of getting rid of their own discomfort, even if it comes at the cost of someone else's mental peace.

Let me share with you a classic example of projection that I witnessed a while back in one of my couples therapy sessions. The couple started arguing at some point because of an incident. The argument itself isn't of much importance in this context, but the way in which the husband tried to get one up on his wife told me a lot about their dynamic. He said in a quiet, almost hissing voice, "After spending 12 years with you, I know you much better than you think you know yourself. And you're pathetic! You'd make up any lies to prove your point!" At that moment, the wife was shocked, but her body language told me that she believed this judgment. Though, a moment ago, she was trying her best to explain her point, now her shoulders drooped and she seemed to give up.

Of course, I had to intervene there, and the husband wasn't all too happy about it. But I want you to pay attention to the husband's strategy here. The moment his wife started presenting valid arguments that disproved his, he felt distinctly uncomfortable that his lies were coming undone. So, what was the best way to shut down this whole conversation? Yes, it was to accuse the other person of lying even though he was the one doing so. Note that he didn't simply make an accusation. He made sure to roll that juicy accusation in the delicious batter of a hurtful and directly personal comment, fried it in the oil of his confident, superior, judgmental attitude, then served it when the wife was least expecting it.

That's one way in which a narcissist uses projection to shock and confuse their victims. This isn't the behavior of someone who loves his wife but rather that of a competitor who must win at all costs. In this case, the cost was his wife's self-esteem and peace of mind. If they'd been allowed to go unchecked, these comments could even have led to the loss of her mental stability. The hopeful piece in this story was that the wife wanted her husband to come to therapy to help her with her depression problems. Had she not pushed for therapy, she'd never have been free of his emotional brutality.

Again, this projection can happen in many different contexts—from parent–child relationships, spouses, and friends to professional acquaintances. The trick is to be able to distinguish between your own emotions and opinions and those being projected onto you. If you aren't careful about this distinction, it can mess with your self-esteem in a big way. Take a look at a few of the most common projections:

- cheating accusations

- labeling the victim as hostile or angry

- declaring their own insecurities to be those of their victim

- claiming manipulation at the hands of the victim

- blaming the victim for bringing the consequences upon themself

Stonewalling

Think of stonewalling as a much more intense version of an abuser's silent treatment. You may even see these two terms used interchangeably. However, there's a fine line between the two when it comes to emotional abuse. While the silent treatment is often used as a form of punishment, stonewalling may be used as a provocation or even as a means of avoiding responsibility by the narcissistic abuser. A stonewalling abuser refuses to participate in communication about certain topics that make them uncomfortable.

For instance, a narcissist may shut down a conversation that questions their accountability in some way. They may say something like, "I'm not talking about that," and simply walk out. Now, this mustn't be confused with someone taking a breather from an escalating situation to allow them to respond more appropriately in time. That's not what a narcissistic abuser does. Instead, this is the tactic they use to silence any uncomfortable conversations.

You may think this isn't as bad as actively abusing or berating someone, but don't be so sure about that just yet. Remember that stonewalling has a cumulative effect on the relationship and on the abused individual. Over time, the victim learns that any sensitive topic will be met with this stonewalling pattern. They're then left with two options: They can either be prepared to be shut down, possibly followed by an emotional outburst from their abuser, or suppress the concerns and not upset the status quo at all. This constant filtering of information to not *upset* your abuser can be distressing, especially when you feel like you can't be yourself in front of them.

Moreover, the abuser's unilateral mandates about what can or cannot be discussed often let them off the hook by simply circumventing any possible talks that would hold them accountable. Remember that, for a narcissistic abuser, the relationship doesn't have much significance beyond being a narcissistic supply anyway. And what better way to do away with the responsibilities of a relationship than to stonewall any uncomfortable situations?

This can be particularly heart-wrenching for someone who struggles with abandonment issues. A person who deeply fears abandonment (more so than regular folks) goes to great lengths to ensure they don't trigger their abuser. This continues the toxic dynamic of strengthening the abuser while the victim withers away in anxiety about all the things they can *never* put out on the table for discussion. They're frozen in a prison-like limbo in their relationship that they can seemingly never get past. Being in limbo isn't really living; it's merely existing.

Shifting Goalposts

Constantly shifting goalposts are yet another terribly frustrating tactic used by abusers. The abuser's expectations and demands change so frequently that it's impossible for the victim to keep up. This greatly contributes to the climate of uncertainty and insecurity in the relationship, since the victim never knows what to expect. No matter how hard the victim tries to anticipate what the abuser may want from them, they cannot. This leaves them in a perpetual state of anxiety over failing to reach a goal they were never informed about in the first place. The goal line is moved and changed without any notice. It's a game with a rulebook the victim isn't allowed to see and where the points system changes on the whim of the abuser. It's rigged such that the victim can never win. For instance, the abuser may first demand that the victim spend time with them. However, when the victim makes plans to do things with the abuser, the latter may accuse them of not giving them enough space. The result is that the victim always falls short, creating a sense of anxiety, confusion, frustration, and hurt.

Earlier, I spoke about a common question that people ask: why the victim doesn't leave. The same question pops up in this regard, too: "If someone makes you feel like a failure all the time, then why would anyone stay in a relationship like that?" Unfortunately, emotional abusers are brilliant at keeping their victims hooked. It's the same principle that keeps people going back to buy lottery tickets despite losing over and over. The thing is, even if you lose ten times but win a dollar the next time, you still go back *hoping* to win something more significant the next time.

Narcissistic abusers use what's called "breadcrumbing" to keep their victims coming back. Ever noticed how a puppy will follow you around if you leave them a trail of treats, even if they don't know you? That's exactly what breadcrumbing is. Abusers leave a trail of *just enough* kindness and care that keeps their victims hoping and trying for more. For example, a self-absorbed narcissist who's been verbally abusive toward his wife for weeks may just decide to leave her a tiny breadcrumb by taking her out for a romantic dinner. He'll make his wife feel special for just the amount of time that suits him and then go back to his abusive patterns.

Remember that this isn't the same as making any real effort to change. Instead, it's just a calculated pattern to manipulate the victim into believing there's hope for the relationship after all. It's this hope that keeps the victim pursuing the abuser despite multiple failures to meet their frequently changing standards. Over time, the victim may feel trapped in a vicious circle of self-doubt and hope for validation. They find themself chasing after a phantom love from a source from which they can never receive it.

Boundary Violations

Boundaries tend to be an extremely touchy topic for emotional abusers. They likely perceive them as an affront to their self-esteem (known as "narcissistic injury") and may even react with retaliation. While setting boundaries is a prescribed measure that ensures psychological well-being in most circumstances, it doesn't work in the case of narcissistic abuse. This is because no matter how many boundaries you set, the abuser always finds a way to cross them. Setting boundaries can even cause some significant backlash from the abuser. They might gaslight you into believing *you're* the one who's controlling and abusive.

When you think about it, this blatant disregard for others' expressed boundaries is quite core to the personality of a narcissistic abuser. For healthy individuals, boundaries are a means of respecting the other individual. However, this basic respect is nonexistent in a narcissist's dictionary. After all, in their minds, no one but themself is deserving of any respect. So, even when you state the things you're uncomfortable with and explicitly ask them not to do those things, they'll still go ahead and do them just to see you squirm with discomfort. For instance, if you tell a narcissistic partner that you'd like them to stop making jokes about your intelligence in front of their family, they might agree and even promise you it won't happen again. However, when the time comes, they do exactly what you requested them not to. At that point, they may say it was all in good humor and not a big deal. They may even mock you for being stuck-up and melodramatic.

Needless to say, these boundary violations are damaging in that they create a sense of fear and insecurity. It's a waiting game in which the victim just waits around to see the next discomfort the narcissist chooses to pick on. It's also worth noting that the victims may eventually get to a point where they no longer bother setting boundaries because it only brings them more pain and suffering.

However, what the victims must understand is this: Even though it's impossible to make an abuser respect their boundaries, they themselves can never give up on them. No contact is probably the best way to manage these boundaries, but that's not always possible. For instance, you might be risking your career if you decide to implement a no-contact policy with your narcissistic boss. In these situations, using a special nonengagement technique known as "gray-rocking" may do the trick. The idea here is to make yourself so uninteresting and unengaging (like a gray rock) that the narcissist just cannot get their supply from you. Now, this technique comes with many caveats of its own and must be used with caution. We'll discuss it in more detail in Part II, where we explore how to recover from this kind of emotional abuse.

Name-Calling and Verbal Assault

Narcissists thrive on drama, and name-calling is one of their favorite tools to fuel that drama. Name-calling is when someone, intentionally or unintentionally, flings demeaning, insulting, and hurtful labels at you. If you've ever been called stupid, ugly, a failure, a good-for-nothing, or endless other negative names, you've been subjected to name-calling—and, let's face it, most of us have faced this at some point or another. It can be traumatizing even if it happens only once, but can you imagine what it would do to your psyche if you had to face it every day?

The worst thing about this kind of name-calling is the double jeopardy it comes with. On one level, the narcissist directly attacks your self-esteem by picking an insecurity they very well know will impact you deeply. Let's say you make the mistake of sharing your deep fear that your colleagues don't really think you deserved your promotion and doubt your caliber. The abuser will use this information you shared in confidence at a work party to call you dumb and stupid. This isn't where it ends, though. On the second level, they'll gaslight you into thinking you're the one who doesn't know how to take a joke. Now, not only is your self-esteem wounded, but you also start wondering if you're actually being overly sensitive. Pay attention to how this also feeds into the boundary-violation tactic in this instance.

Similar to stonewalling, name-calling also allows the abuser to deflect any responsibility. It's natural for you to want to defend yourself when they call you all these berating names. However, all this does is give the abuser a "get out of jail free" card, because now the argument is all about you trying to defend yourself and them gaslighting you all over again.

Restrictions

Narcissistic abusers follow a systematic blueprint to restrict their victims' social, financial, and occupational lives. These restrictions may be veiled as care and concern in the beginning, but in reality they're just a means of coercive control. For example, if a woman has a demanding job, an abusive partner may "lovingly" tell her, "Hey, you know what? I feel like your job keeps you away from me for too long. I think you should leave that job. And I make enough money for the both of us anyway. I just want you to relax and enjoy this new life with me." During the love-bombing, idealizing stage, it may be hard to find fault with this logic. So, the woman may give up her career in terms of both income and ambition. It may be a little late by the time she realizes this was a meticulous ruse to restrict her freedom. It also closes the door to her ever being able to leave him, especially if she has children she needs to support. He's basically blocking her path of escape from him, making it nearly impossible for her to survive without his income.

It's interesting to note, however, that these restrictions aren't always placed that directly. More often than not, the narcissist will get you to do things without actually telling you to do them. One of my clients, Casey, narrated an incident that highlights this point perfectly. She'd been dealing with an abusive husband for years before she decided to break free and divorce him. As she was healing herself, for some sense of closure, she decided to analyze the chain of events by which he'd removed all her social supports with almost clinical precision.

Casey recalled a particular series of events with one of her close friends, Janet, including this one double date she and her husband went on with Janet and her husband that, somehow, became their last encounter. Casey and her now ex had recently got hitched and had just received the news that they were pregnant the morning of the date. Casey was obviously happy to share this news with Janet when she saw her. The rest of the dinner was uneventful, full of small talk, jokes, and, in general, a good time. When they returned home, however, her husband had an agenda. He'd seemed ticked off right from the moment they walked out of the restaurant and got into their car, in fact. He went on and on about how Janet's husband was such a show-off, how Janet herself seemed like a gold-digger, and whatnot! Casey, though confused by these judgments, didn't argue because she knew her ex was having a tough time at work, having been passed over for a promotion.

But as they entered their home, her husband made a peculiar remark that began the cycle of isolation. He said, "Did you notice Janet's reaction when you announced the baby news? She obviously wasn't happy!" When Casey thought back, she realized that Janet had maybe not been as excited as she'd have liked—though in retrospect, Casey understood that there may have been other reasons for the lack of excitement. As she recalled this story in therapy, she believed that the lukewarm reaction was probably because Casey hadn't been spending enough time with Janet prior to that dinner because her relationship was taking up so much of her energy. Or it could have been simply because Janet just didn't like Casey's then husband and was worried about her. Yet, in that moment, her husband succeeded in planting the seeds of doubt in Casey's mind.

These seeds were then watered and nurtured every time Janet's name came up. Casey's husband would say something like, "Ugh, I just don't trust her," or "I bet she's just jealous of you." And, slowly, Casey stopped being in touch with her altogether. So, even though she hadn't been *instructed* to stop talking to Janet, she'd obviously been manipulated into it. This happened with regard to all her friends and family, until one day she realized she had no one left but this abusive husband. To top it off, he even had the audacity to say she didn't have any friends because she was so selfish.

Now, you may wonder why a narcissist would spend so much time and energy isolating their victim. The reason is simple: to protect their supply. They're scared that the people who care about their victim may expose the narcissist and their manipulations. Moreover, if the victim has their loved ones around them, it's easier for them to just leave—and that's not acceptable to a narcissist.

Flying Monkeys

If you've watched *The Wizard of Oz*, you'll be able to compare the flying monkeys referred to in narcissistic abuse to the winged monkeys of Oz. In this beloved tale, these monkeys are mischievous creatures who do the Wicked Witch's bidding. The concept remains the same here: The narcissistic abuser knows how to corner you from all sides, and when they can't do it all on their own, they recruit others who do their bidding.

Now, these flying monkeys come in two varieties—those who are themselves victims of the narcissist's lies and manipulation, and those who may share some, if not all, of the abuser's narcissistic traits. These flying monkeys often propagate the narcissist's version of reality, thereby gaslighting the victim on a whole new level. They do this in many different ways:

- **Spreading rumors:** Flying monkeys work in the same sneaky ways a narcissist does. They're so enamored by the narcissist's version of reality that they'll go to any extent to defame the victim. They'll tell people twisted lies that make the whole situation more distressing for the victim. This is often seen in workplaces, where the flying monkeys may flock together to create what almost seems like an alternative reality, where the victim is blamed and the abuser is portrayed as the victim. This is often done to garner favors from an abuser who's in a superior position.

- **Keeping tabs on the victim:** The flying monkeys also serve as the abuser's surveillance team, gathering information about the victim and supplying it back to the abuser. This information often plays a massive role in sustaining the abuser's control over the victim's psyche. In their sneaky surveillance, these flying monkeys may very well discover evidence that proves the narcissist's abuse. However, they're either so brainwashed or so driven by their own narcissistic motives that they simply discard the evidence and continue to bolster the abuser's version of events.

- **Trivializing the victim's perspective:** Some flying monkeys may not do the victim outright harm but may try to change their perception of the abuse itself. Most commonly, they tell the victim that what they're experiencing isn't a big deal, that they're blowing it out of proportion, and even that everyone experiences these circumstances at some point. Below, we talk about minimization as one of the narcissist's tactics too, but a flying monkey's minimization may be much less obvious than that of a narcissist.

Remember that these flying monkeys are often people who know both the victim and the abuser. A narcissist carefully recruits these people to meticulously isolate the victim even further.

Minimization

By now, you know that a narcissist will tell you about themselves every chance they get while completely diminishing your experiences. And yet, their minimization can come at the most unexpected times and in the most shocking ways. Of course, your shock and hurt are the exact supply the abuser is looking for in these situations. Understanding the different ways in which they minimize your experiences is crucial to coping with this abusive tactic.

Sure, there's the obvious minimization, where they'll invalidate your feelings without a second thought. They'll tell you things like, "You're overreacting," "You're being too sensitive," or even "I didn't mean to tell them your secret; it just came out in the flow of the conversation. I didn't think you'd mind." However, that's not all there is to minimization—it can take on much subtler forms, such as snubbing you into believing you're worthless. Here are a couple of not-so-obvious and yet just as hurtful minimization instances I've seen in my practice over the years:

- **Accusing you of being a show-off:** The narcissist absolutely hates it when they aren't the ones in the spotlight. Anytime you share wonderful news, they'll try all kinds of tactics to get that spotlight off you.

  One of my clients who taught kids piano spoke about her always-mocking husband. Once, he said he couldn't figure out why all these parents were paying her just for talking to their kids and playing some scales and songs. These passing remarks took away the quiet pride she felt in being a music teacher.

  She reported that one morning, after they'd separated, she was sitting at her kitchen table and heard the garage door going up. When it was her oldest son who walked in the door instead of her husband, she relaxed. She hadn't realized she'd been so tense every time she thought he was home. She remembered steeling herself not to tell him anything good that had happened that day. She said, "He wanted to take away everything good in my life. He would find something wrong with it."

  For instance, she reported that when she'd had a wonderful time with her friend going shopping in an old part of a nearby town, he told her that everyone who saw them walking down the street probably thought they were a lesbian couple since her friend had a spiky haircut. This told her that he was determined to steal her joy *and* that he was a homophobe, which she found despicable. Even after their divorce, he'd lie about her to their children occasionally, but they never paid him any attention because they themselves had witnessed the truth of the abuse their mother was subjected to.

- **Claiming you're an inconvenience:** If there's one thing you must know about emotional abusers, it's that they know how to kick you when you're down—emotionally, of course. Take a look at an incident narrated by a cancer survivor in one of our sessions. She thought of her cancer journey as a blessing in disguise because it showed her how strong she was and how emotionally abusive her so-called loving ex-husband was. She remembered the physical pain and the emotional distress of her chemo sessions quite vividly. But nothing seemed to shake her as much as the memories of her ex's emotional abuse.

  Her then husband would repeatedly make passing comments about how this cancer diagnosis had become a nuisance for *him*, as he had to drive her back and forth from her treatments, come home to a depressing environment, and not have anyone to take care of his needs. Remember that the world still saw this man as a wonderful husband who was there for his wife through thick and thin. But behind closed doors, these passing remarks had a terrible consequence. Though, now, she sees them as unacceptable, when it was happening this abusive pattern completely broke my client's sense of self-worth. She admits to even having considered ending her life because she simply couldn't bear the feeling of being a burden on her loved ones. This is what emotional abuse can do to a victim.

If you've had firsthand contact with an emotional abuser, you may have encountered one or more of the above tactics in several forms with varying intensities. Awareness of abuse is the first step in healing. Though spotting these tactics in your daily interactions may feel a little overwhelming at first, recognizing them for what they are is an essential step in moving forward in your journey.

Now that you have an understanding of what abuse looks like in general, it's time to learn how to identify it in specific contexts. As mentioned earlier, emotional abuse in the workplace may look very different from emotional abuse within families. The next chapter will help you recognize the subtle and not-so-subtle differences.

Chapter 3:

The Different Faces of Abuse

The human brain is wired to prefer neat and clean categories of objects as opposed to the chaos of possibilities. This is why most people view abuse through an almost limiting lens. In their minds, something can be considered abuse only if certain people in certain places and in certain ways try to harm another individual. What they don't understand is that abuse is just as complex as the humans involved. This means there are no limits to who abuses someone, the where, or the how.

We looked at the "how" part of abuse in the previous chapter; now, let's take a deeper look at where this abuse may take place. As you go through this chapter, I want you to keep the abuser's tactics at the back of your mind so you can gain a much clearer sense of the practical nature of abuse as it unfolds around you.

The only way to truly understand abuse is to view it from all possible vantage points and at all possible levels. Without this all-encompassing perspective, it's easy to fall into the trap of wanting to put the idea of abuse into a neatly wrapped box. Unfortunately, this only prevents you from healing. Here, we categorize abuse in terms of the different settings and relationships in which it may occur, the different kinds of victims the abuser may target, and, lastly, the different tools they may use to perpetrate abuse. Elaborate discussions on each of these could be separate books in themselves, so the idea here is to give you a brief overview of what abuse would look like in these situations.

Abuse in Different Relationships

Until now, though we haven't discussed them explicitly, most of the examples we've used have been in the context of what you might call "conventional" relationships. It must be emphasized, however, that abuse isn't exclusive to these so-called conventional couples. Below are a couple of relationship contexts we must pay special attention to.

Abuse in Same-Sex Relationships

Ideas about gender and abuse are so entangled in the social discourse that it's almost impossible for many people to imagine the possibility of abuse in same-sex relationships: "If gender and power dynamics are balanced, then who abuses whom in the relationship?" Well, same-sex relationships are an excellent reminder that abuse sees no gender, stature, or appearance, or even feminine or masculine characteristics. While all of the previously discussed abusive tactics may also be present in same-sex relationships, the social context often makes things a lot more complex. Consider the following instances that are specific to emotional abuse in same-sex relationships:

- **Biased social outlook:** One of the biggest issues that arises in abusive same-sex relationships is the homophobic or transphobic attitudes of the people around the couple. The abusive partner may leverage these attitudes to prevent the victim from leaving. For instance, if the victim hasn't explicitly come out to their family, friends, colleagues, or employers, the abuser may threaten to out them if they leave. Furthermore, these phobic views may make it a lot easier for the abuser to isolate their victim socially, as they may already have a limited social support system.

  On another level, it's also important to remember that both partners in a same-sex relationship may have similar experiences of discrimination and abuse outside the relationship—from their families, employers, or other social institutions. This shared suffering is often reflected in the excuses the victim makes for their partner's abuse: "She didn't mean to slap me. She's been very frustrated with her boss's discriminatory behavior and just didn't know what to do with all that pent-up anger. Unfortunately, I just happened to be there."

  In many same-sex relationships, the abuse springs from the abuser's own homophobia or transphobia. The abuser themself may not have come out to the world. They may deny their sexuality in social contexts while berating the victim and telling them they deserve to be abused. They may even discourage the victim from reaching out for help by convincing them that social workers, police, and therapists are also homophobic or transphobic. The point is that the single issue of homophobia and transphobia can manifest in several different ways in same-sex relationships, making it easier for the abuser to perpetrate their manipulative tactics.

- **Questioning the validity of the partner's experience:** In same-sex couples, gaslighting may be taken a notch higher, with the abuser questioning the very sexuality of the victim. They may invalidate their experiences, accusing them of faking to gain sympathy. For example, a lesbian woman who hangs out with male friends may be called disrespectful names by her abusive partner. They may also ridicule the victim's desire to seek help by questioning who would believe their stories of abuse in a same-sex relationship.

- **A limited number of role models:** Victims from the LGBTQ community are less likely to have inspiring role models who've left abusive relationships behind. This may lead them to believe that staying in an abusive relationship is better than being alone. This may be especially the case if the thought of leaving triggers deep abandonment issues that they've faced due to their sexuality.

While many of these issues have a societal layer, they all contribute to complicating emotional abuse in same-sex couples.

Abuse in Polyamorous and Nontraditional Relationships

Contrary to what some people may believe, polyamorous relationships are not arbitrarily less moral than traditional monogamous relationships. They are also not the same as cheating, the most critical distinguishing factor between the two being consent. Though a polyamorous relationship doesn't automatically translate to an abusive one, it must be noted that such relationships may put the people involved in uniquely vulnerable situations. The reason for this is simple: Since these relationships don't subscribe to traditional norms, there may be quite a big gray area as to what a healthy, loving relationship should look like. This often works in the favor of a narcissistic abuser, who exploits the lack of boundaries to perpetrate abusive behaviors.

It's a given that trust is indispensable for any polyamorous relationship to work. However, an abuser can manipulate their victims a great deal by violating their trust. Consider the following ways in which abuse can spill into these kinds of relationships:

- The abuser may want to be polygamous but wants their partner to stay monogamous.

- The abuser may pressure their partner to open up the relationship.

- They may want to transition into polyamory because they've cheated and then gaslight the victim into thinking that it's something they, the victim, did.

Abuse in Different Settings

Just as different kinds of relationships are vulnerable to different kinds of abuse, so are different kinds of settings. Here, let's discuss three of the most common settings that are prone to emotional abuse.

Workplace Abuse

Many people will tell you that workplace abuse is nothing but a new-age term that younger people use when they want to sound dramatic: "After all, if someone's paying you to get the work done, then what's the big deal if they use strict measures to ensure you do the work?" Let's start by clarifying that workplace abuse isn't the same as setting rigorous performance standards. It's also not the same as not getting along with your colleagues or boss.

Instead, a workplace becomes toxic when shame and blame become the primary modes of functioning. You start dreading going to work every day, and fear becomes the only currency of workplace exchanges. Workplace abuse can not only make you doubt your abilities and performance at work but also impact your life outside the workplace. Anxiety in the form of loss of appetite, sleeplessness, and even social withdrawal is quite common among victims. Here's what emotional abuse can look like in the workplace:

- **A climate of intimidation:** A narcissistic boss knows how to use verbal abuse to create a culture of insecurity and terror in the workplace. They may do this by either threatening you openly with termination or using more subtle ways of making your life difficult. Remember stonewalling from the previous chapter? Turns out it's the narcissist's favorite tool in the workplace too. For instance, they may promptly shut down their victim's ideas and pitches with unwarranted criticism and sarcasm. Sometimes, they may move on to others without even acknowledging their victim's suggestions. As in the personal context, being treated like this in front of colleagues can feel especially insulting and demeaning.

- **Passive-aggressive tactics:** The abuser and their flying monkeys may create a workplace environment that feels extremely unsafe by spreading rumors about the target's personal life; they may even gossip about intimate details the victim has shared with them in confidence. These details are often used to cast aspersions, not only over the victim's professional capabilities but also over their very character and worth. At this point, the victim may themself withdraw from any kind of social interaction at work. However, if that doesn't happen, the abuser may go one step further and actively isolate the victim from the rest of the team by not informing them about the time and venue of team meetings, withholding details about team activities, and so on. These passive-aggressive tactics may not seem like much on paper, but when they happen to you every other day, they can suck the life energy right out of you.

- **Physical advances:** The final intimidation tactic may be sexual harassment and inappropriate advances. While some of these may be obvious, others may not be. For example, cracking tasteless jokes at the expense of someone's gender may be the first rung of a long ladder of harassment.

Digital Abuse

There's no doubt that technology has transformed our lives completely. Whether it's access to tremendous amounts of knowledge and information or the ability to connect with our loved ones regardless of the distance that separates us, technological tools such as search engines and social media have made our lives so much easier. However, not many people realize that, on the flip side, this digital transformation often comes at the price of giving abusers easy access to exploitative tools.

Digital abuse uses technology to harass, isolate, and intimidate victims. An example of this could be an abusive partner stalking and tracking your movements using your smartphone's GPS location or an ex using texts, emails, instant messaging, and social media platforms to send threatening messages to their victim.

Digital platforms may also offer a means of harassing a victim without ever meeting them in person. For example, abuse in the form of cyberbullying may be carried out with the abuser having no contact with their victim outside of the online platforms. Think of online gaming rooms as an example, where the victim is constantly trolled and shamed. Online grooming and predatory behavior are an example of how an adult, or even a young teen, may be lured into dating solely through digital means with no physical contact in the beginning. Even financial abuse through digital hacking would fall into this category. In other words, technology becomes the abuser's weapon of choice to manipulate the targeted individual emotionally, sexually, financially, and so on. Regardless of whether it's a known or unknown entity perpetrating the digital abuse, the consequences can be massively debilitating for the victim.

Spiritual Abuse

Any attempts to dominate or control an individual using faith or religion amount to spiritual abuse. This kind of abuse may be perpetrated by either a religious leader in the context of a religious group or a known individual from your social circle. As you can imagine, the two manifest in very different ways.

Spiritual abuse by a religious leader may look something like as follows:

- quoting scriptures to criticize and humiliate you

- coercing you to be intimate

- making you feel obligated to donate money and other resources or to do things you aren't comfortable doing

On the other hand, spiritual abuse in a personal setting may look like this:

- ridiculing your religious beliefs and practices

- leveraging religious beliefs to manipulate and exploit you

- using religious texts to justify abuse

- encroaching on others' freedom to choose their own religion

This kind of abuse can completely wreck the victim's belief system and hamper their ability to effectively cope with challenging situations in life, as their coping mechanism of faith is shaken.

Abuse With Different Victims

So far, our focus has largely been on the adult section of the population. Now let's focus on two particularly vulnerable groups that may not always be able to reach out for support.

Child Abuse

Whenever I talk about child emotional abuse, there's at least one person who says something like, "But we grew up with some pretty harsh parenting, and we turned out fine!" Even if we concede that they have turned out fine (which most often they haven't; they usually have a lot of suppressed emotional issues), I urge them to think about their relationship with their parents, and they immediately realize what this so-called "harsh parenting" does to the parent–child dynamic.

Most emotionally abused children, like Katherine from the Introduction, grow up with one of two beliefs: They either believe the abuse to be a form of parental love ("They just want what's best for me!") or they grow up believing they're unworthy of love ("There must be something wrong with me!"). They may never realize that they were the victim of a narcissistic abuser trying to fulfill their own needs rather than thinking about the needs of the child.

Child emotional abuse can manifest in several ways, each unleashing a different kind of impact on the child's psyche. All of the abuser's tactics—such as triangulation, projection, name-calling, shifting goalposts, and minimization—may be seen in parent–child relationships. However, two tactics we must consider in addition to the previously discussed ones are neglect and withholding affection.

Emotional neglect is when the caregiver refuses to give validation, attention, and emotional support to a child. Remember that a child is looking for all of these things because they're the building blocks with which they build their sense of self-worth and identity. Think of a healthy sense of self as a sapling and validation, attention, and support as the sunlight, soil, and water. Without these things, the sapling will never turn into a healthy plant. Children who have been denied them often grow into adults who either desperately seek validation from friends and partners or cannot form any healthy attachments.

A dangerous manifestation of this neglect is the withholding of affection. As in Katherine's case, the child may feel compelled to strive for the abusive parent's approval, which never comes. The result is that the child constantly pursues approval while the parent willfully starves the child of what they most need. The child's experience of frustration and confusion is often similar to that of gaslit victims and results in a perpetual sense of rejection.

The sad reality is, even though neglect is one of the most emotionally harmful forms of child abuse, it is still one of the most difficult to recognize. Therefore, the odds of an abused child receiving help in time are quite low, and the child may begin to heal from the abuse only when they become an adult.

Abuse of the Elderly

Elder abuse is the intentional mistreatment of older adults in the form of neglect, physical abuse, financial exploitation, and abandonment. Elders with medical conditions that restrict their movement or who require the help of caretakers for basic tasks are often at risk of such abuse. This is especially true when they have a limited social support system. Consider the following indicators that may help others recognize abuse that's happening behind closed doors:

- sudden unexplained weight loss

- unexplained bruises and injuries

- social withdrawal

- sudden financial degradation

- restricted access to medical necessities

- deterioration of overall physical and mental health

A critical aspect of preventing such abuse is education and awareness. This may include encouraging older people to have their legal documents, such as a will and healthcare power of attorney, in place. It also involves educating them about financial best practices, such as maintaining secrecy of information about their accounts, tracking financial transactions, and so on.

Abuse With Different Tools

Last but not least, we come to the master manipulator's tools of choice that they use to create a culture of insecurity, fear, and doubt wherever they go. Any discussion on abuse would be incomplete without understanding the means that an abuser frequently uses to isolate their victims. We've already mentioned these in passing, but let's zero in on them to understand exactly what they mean.

Physical Abuse

Physical abuse is easy to understand for most people due to the presence of clear physical aggression. Any intentional bodily injury as a result of violence may be termed physical abuse. This can include anything from slapping, shoving, and restraining to the inappropriate administration of drugs to keep the victim under control. However, what many don't realize is that physical abuse is more than just physical harm. For instance, behaviors like smashing objects or punching walls are also forms of physical abuse that are intended to intimidate and manipulate the victim in some way.

Many people think physical and emotional abuse are two distinct categories that belong in separate boxes. For instance, a victim may say something like, "I know he has a bad temper and sometimes he loses control over his words, but he'd never *do* anything to hurt me." However, research suggests that verbal abuse is often a predictor of physical violence to come (Brewster, 2000). Here are a few early signs that may warn you of physical abuse in the future (Vevers, 2023):

- possessiveness

- hypersensitivity

- unrealistic and rigid gender role expectations

- pushing for the relationship to progress more quickly than you're comfortable with

- aggressive behaviors, including throwing or breaking objects, threatening violence against pets or children, pinning the victim to the floor or against the wall, and so on

- isolation

You'll notice that all of these predictors are the exact same behaviors we discussed as part of the abuser's playbook. The lesson, therefore, is that an abuser's manipulative methods are often just the beginning of a slippery slope that leads to dangerous physical confrontations.

Financial Abuse

The financial angle holds a unique place in the big picture of abuse. The short version is obviously that the abuser assumes all control over the victim's finances, thereby preventing them from making any independent financial decisions. Condemning this pattern is an easy choice for most. After all, every individual should have the right to make their own financial choices, right? However, the longer version is where this seemingly clear-cut line blurs just a tad—let's see how.

Financial abuse may involve restrictions such as not allowing the victim to access their own bank accounts, withholding a basic allowance from them, monitoring their spending extremely closely, forcing them to take credit or loans in the abuser's name, and so on. However, many people do not realize that this financial abuse is frequently a part of wider economic abuse. Economic abuse occurs when the abuser controls not only how the victim spends their money but also their means of earning it. For instance, a narcissistic abuser, in an attempt to isolate their victim, may force them to leave their job or give up on their education. This not only creates an immediate dependency on the abuser but also weakens the victim's resolve (and ability) to leave the abusive situation in the future.

Even though, on paper, this seems like an unacceptable way to control the victim, it may not always appear so in real life. When this kind of economic and financial abuse begins, it's often taken as a sign of loving behavior, especially in an intimate relationship: "My boyfriend doesn't want me to commute at odd times; that's why he doesn't want me to go to university. He's very protective of me, you see!" It's only much later that the victim realizes the cumulative damage of the so-called protectiveness, not only to their mental health but also to their economic circumstances. This financial isolation allows the abuser to use money as a form of reward and punishment, which can leave a deep gash in the victim's sense of self-worth.

It's important to note that though we've segregated the forms of abuse into different categories, in real life there will undoubtedly be frequent and substantial overlap between them. Therefore, it becomes important to focus on the indicators of abuse that a victim experiences rather than trying to label the type of abuse it is. Moreover, acknowledging these experiences and the negative impact the abuse has on the victim's well-being often becomes the first step in their recovery. We'll try to understand this impact in more detail in the next chapter.

Chapter 4:

Decoding the Damage Unleashed by the Abuser

In the 1950s, a psychologist named Leon Festinger did a series of experiments in which the subjects were required to complete some extremely dull and monotonous tasks (Leder, 2021). Once they'd completed the tasks, the researcher would enter the room and ask them to tell the next participant how fun and exciting the tasks were. The next participant, however, was also a researcher, who was only pretending to be a participant in the study. This researcher would then record the subject's account, unbeknownst to them.

Here's where the brilliance of this experiment lay: The subjects were divided into two groups, one of which was paid $1 and the other $20. The researchers wanted to know which group would present their views more enthusiastically.

Now, you may think the answer would be obvious. If both groups had to lie about the experiment being fun, the group that received a higher amount of money would have to be the one that lied more enthusiastically, right? Well, the experimenters consistently found the exact opposite: The $1 group was substantially more enthused about the task than the $20 group. The experimenters explained these counterintuitive results with the help of a psychological phenomenon known as cognitive dissonance.

Cognitive dissonance is the discomfort we all feel when our actions and behaviors don't match our beliefs and attitudes. The $20 group believed that the amount they were paid was reasonable enough for them to lie. On the other hand, the $1 group just couldn't find enough reasons to justify their lying. So, the fact that they'd lied about a boring task without even being given enough money for doing so created a conflict between the way they'd felt and the way they'd acted.

The only way this conflict could be resolved was by either changing their actions and speaking the truth about the tasks or changing their own perception about the dullness of the tasks. Festinger found, in his series of experiments, that most people chose to change their own thinking to align their behaviors and beliefs rather than change their behaviors.

Now, I'm sure you're wondering: *Why on earth are we talking about this random experiment in a book about abuse?!* Well, it turns out that this phenomenon called cognitive dissonance is at the core of emotional abuse. For instance, a narcissistic abuser may use the good old gaslighting tactic to create cognitive dissonance between the victim's reality and the reality they want the victim to believe. This discrepancy often leads the victim to minimize their own thoughts and feelings rather than leave the abusive relationship. Yes, there are times when a victim will actually change their own beliefs about reality and go against their own knowledge of the truth rather than leave the relationship!

You don't need me to tell you that abuse damages your self-esteem. However, there's more to it than that generalized statement. This chapter helps you understand the specific ways in which abuse can impact you, including triggering several mental health conditions. Taking stock of this impact is critical before we move on to healing and recovery from abuse in Part II.

Impact of Abuse on Your Physical Health

There's no doubt that being emotionally abused over the long term has significant health risks. There are two facets to these risks—the brain and the body:

- **Brain changes:** Research evidence suggests that childhood abuse is largely responsible for certain brain changes in the specific regions associated with understanding and controlling emotions and recognizing and responding to the feelings of others (Heim et al., 2013). The researchers reported a thinning of the brain tissue involved in self-awareness and emotional regulation. These changes often make affected individuals susceptible to negative emotions and moods, making them focus on the painful memories of abuse, which in turn makes them vulnerable to depression, anxiety, low self-esteem, moodiness, and extreme or dulled emotional responses. So, anyone who thinks emotional abuse doesn't do any "real" harm needs to rethink their perspective.

- **Bodily conditions:** Have you ever seen a cat backed up in a corner—arched back, fur standing upright, and ready to pounce? That posture is an indicator that the cat feels threatened and stressed. Humans have a similar fight-or-flight response in which their nervous system prepares their body for what's perceived as an oncoming battle. The brain releases a hormone called cortisol, also known as the "stress hormone," which signals to different bodily systems that they must now work at an accelerated pace. For instance, the heart must pump more blood, the muscles must tense up for the anticipated action, and so on. However, once the stressor vanishes from the environment, the brain stops releasing this hormone, so your bodily systems can now relax and settle back into a comfortable rhythm. Now, think about what would happen if your body was placed under such stress all the time without being given the time to recuperate. Consistently high levels of cortisol in the bloodstream may result in several health complications, such as weight gain, elevated blood pressure and blood sugar levels, muscle aches, arthritis, and so on (Cleveland Clinic, n.d.-a; Polinski et al., 2019).

For many people, the impact of abuse suddenly seems like a very real thing the moment they hear about these bodily consequences. However, it's important to note that these complications are only the tip of the iceberg. You simply cannot gauge the extent of the impact of abuse without knowing what it does to a person's mental health.

Abuse and Mental Health

Any kind of abuse, whether emotional or physical, is undoubtedly a means of gaining power over another individual, and this endeavor is simply impossible without wounding the victim's sense of self. This can be a trigger for several mental health conditions. Now that you understand how your body's stress system operates, it's not surprising that victims of emotional abuse may struggle with mental health concerns such as depression and anxiety (Tian et al., 2023; Liu et al., 2023). However, other comorbid diagnoses may complicate matters further.

Eating Disorders

A significant amount of research has centered around childhood abuse and eating disorders. While a large chunk of this research focuses specifically on sexual abuse, emotional abuse has also been reported by several participants as a strong risk factor (Robinson et al., 2024). For instance, author David Royse reports a study in his book *Emotional Abuse of Children* in which a staggering 81% of women with bulimia-spectrum disorders reported having been emotionally abused as children (Royse, 2016).

Of course, you don't need statistics to see the havoc that abuse can wreak on someone's self-esteem. Imagine this scenario: A woman who's just given birth comes into therapy reporting consistently low moods and anxiety. Having ruled out postpartum depression, the focus of the sessions then shifts to her relationship with her husband. She mentions that he's been making sly comments about her weight since the pregnancy, saying things like, "Are you sure you want to eat that? All those extra calories you eat have to go somewhere, you know! Pregnancy hasn't done your body any favors as it is!" or "Why can't you maintain yourself like my colleagues' wives?!"

While these comments in themselves are a classic sign of abuse, in this instance they're even more traumatizing for the wife because they remind her of her teenage interactions with her mother. Even though she's never been obese, her mother always gaslit her into believing she was. This resulted in a dysfunctional relationship with food, reflected in her struggle with bulimia prior to the pregnancy. As a teen and young adult, she would indulge in binge eating and then induce vomiting in the hope that the calories wouldn't stick. Although she worked on herself extensively in therapy prior to her pregnancy, her anxieties have now been triggered thanks to her husband's comments. She has the constant urge to use food as a means of filling her emotional emptiness and then inducing vomiting to keep from gaining weight.

You'll notice that these abusive interactions that may trigger eating disorders later in life almost always have their roots in early relationships with primary caregivers. This is because nothing can steal our sense of self like backhanded compliments and cruel, mean-spirited comments from the people we relied on from the moment we came into this world. These abusive remarks often hamper the child's ability to regulate their emotions. The child learns that anytime they display honest emotions, they're likely to get shot down by their abusive parent's anger, sarcasm, or just plain neglect. The child then goes on to suppress these emotions, and as an adult may look to distractions such as food and other substances to divert their attention from the seething negativity within.

Substance Abuse

Understanding substance abuse as a consequence of an abusive environment can be a little difficult, simply because it's often also one of the causes. While on the one hand, dependence on substances can contribute to people lashing out and create a toxic and unstable atmosphere at home, on the other hand, many people engage in substance abuse as a way to numb their own experiences of past abuse. Either way, substance abuse becomes a risk factor that sustains the abusive cycle, often even over generations. Look at the following case to gauge this tremendously complex relationship.

Hugh grew up with an extremely abusive narcissistic father. As a young boy, he remembers feeling intense fear and anger as he and his mother had to constantly walk on eggshells around his father, desperately trying not to upset him. But no matter what they did, something would always tick him off, especially on the days he came home drunk. Though he never physically abused Hugh's mother, Hugh frequently bore the brunt of his father's temper tantrums. Despite the beatings and extreme punishments he received as a child, what Hugh seems to remember with deep bitterness is the verbal venom his father spewed during his rage episodes.

As he grew older, Hugh's hurt, bitterness, and suppressed anger began to haunt him no matter how far he went from his dysfunctional family. He started drinking and smoking to numb the chaos and turmoil in his head. Even though he'd resolved never to be like his father, he found himself falling into those familiar dysfunctional patterns. He would go on cruel rants, calling his wife and their son the worst mistakes of his life, until one day things went too far and the emotional abuse turned physical. Even after his wife left with their son, it took Hugh a very long time to accept that he'd turned into the very abuser he'd been running from all his life, and that his substance dependence had made things all the more complicated.

Complex Post-Traumatic Stress Disorder

While many people have heard of post-traumatic stress disorder (PTSD), they may not be aware of what exactly this condition entails. Here, we'll talk specifically about complex PTSD (c-PTSD), one of the types of PTSD that's quite common among victims of emotional abuse.

PTSD is a clinical diagnosis of a victim's reaction to a traumatic event even after it's passed. The condition may involve symptoms such as vivid reliving of the traumatic experience, recurring nightmares, anxiety, depression, and avoidance behaviors toward places, actions, people, or any other aspects associated with the traumatic event. For instance, a war veteran may have been so traumatized by the scenes they witnessed that they may experience extreme anxiety and flashbacks any time a war scene plays on the TV or someone brings up the topic at a social gathering. The trauma is so intense that it often interferes with their smooth functioning in daily life.

What emotional abuse victims experience may be slightly different. c-PTSD is when an abuse victim experiences many PTSD symptoms in addition to others, such as relationship issues, emotional dysregulation, and a weak sense of self. The main distinguishing factor between PTSD and c-PTSD is the nature of the trauma. While a one-time traumatic experience may cause PTSD, c-PTSD is often the result of exposure to chronic trauma, which is repetitive or continual in nature. The result is that a person with c-PTSD from emotional abuse may feel worthless, guilty, irritable, and sometimes even suicidal, in addition to the regular symptoms of PTSD. These symptoms may compel the individual to withdraw themself from social relationships, which can further worsen their state of mind.

Please be aware that the list of mental health conditions discussed here is by no means exhaustive. These are only the diagnoses that frequently come up in the context of emotional abuse. That being said, just because a victim's lived experience doesn't fulfill particular diagnostic criteria, their experience cannot be trivialized.

The Trap of Trauma Bonding

Leaving an abusive relationship may seem like the most logical thing to do on paper, but abuse victims repeatedly find themselves going back to their abusers as if bound to them by an invisible spell. Trauma bonding with the abuser may just be that invisible spell. A trauma bond is an emotional attachment to the very abuser who makes your life miserable. "But why on earth would you feel anything remotely positive toward someone who berates and ridicules you every chance they get?" you might ask. The mystery can be decoded with the concept of intermittent reinforcement.

In behavioral psychology, the technique of intermittent reinforcement is considered to be the most effective at generating the desired results. Here, a reward is delivered at irregular intervals so the individual performing the task has no idea when their efforts will be rewarded. This results in consistent efforts, driven by the hope that they'll soon be rewarded. Something similar may be at work when it comes to the phenomenon of trauma bonding. Narcissistic abusers are extremely good at stringing along their victims. They love-bomb their victims in such small and unpredictable doses that their victims keep going back to them in the hope of more so-called good moments.

It must be noted, however, that love-bombing may not be the only way in which abusers keep their victims hooked. They may also narrate traumatic incidents from their past and instances of their own victimization. It's these incidents that make the victims rationalize their abusers' actions. For instance, a wife may rationalize her husband's verbal abuse as stemming from his own abuse at the hands of his narcissistic mother. She may even go so far as to excuse his behavior, saying that he's kind, caring, and *almost* perfect more often than not.

Of course, these behavioral exchanges are also backed by certain hormonal changes, which make it hard for the victims to break the trauma bonds. When we face a threat, it's natural for us to turn to those who offer physical or emotional support and protection and the love we need to overcome the threat. When we receive this support, our brain releases oxytocin, also known as the love hormone, further reinforcing the relationship. Unfortunately, in abusive relationships, the person threatening us and the person offering support are one and the same. This makes the relationship even more complicated.

Stockholm Syndrome and Emotional Bonding to the Abuser

When discussing abuse, it's worth exploring the concept of Stockholm syndrome, which is an extreme form of trauma bonding. Even though Stockholm syndrome sounds like a fancy, clinical diagnosis, it's not. Rather, it's simply a name given to the trauma bond that a victim develops with their abuser. It originated from a robbery case in Stockholm in 1973 (Ritter & Olsen, 2023). Criminologist and psychiatrist Nils Bejerot, advising police in this standoff, noticed that some hostages sided with the captors and even went against the police. While Bejerot himself named it Norrmalmstorg syndrome, worldwide it became known as Stockholm syndrome.

To an objective observer, this may seem exactly the same as trauma bonding. However, the victim may tell you a different story. While in regular trauma bonding the abuser may not seem to reciprocate the positive attachment of the victim, in Stockholm syndrome the bond may be perceived as developing from both sides. Let's say a captor threatens their victim with execution if their instructions aren't followed. So, the victim does exactly as they're told and the threat of execution is averted. In fact, they may even receive the basic necessities to keep going. The victim, in this case, may develop positive feelings toward the abuser with rationalizations such as, "They kept their word" or "They really do care for me."

It's almost as if the victim sees the holding back of violence by the abuser as a show of kindness—or sometimes even love. The flip side is that the victim may feel as if the responsibility for the abuse lies with them rather than with their abuser. When the abuse does happen, the victim may blame themself for it by thinking, *Maybe I pushed them to do this; something I did must have hurt or angered them. Maybe I deserve this.*

Again, it's worth noting that these behavioral exchanges unfold in the foreground of certain cognitive processes that happen simultaneously. The two-factor theory of emotions proposed by psychologists Stanley Schachter and Jerome E. Singer in 1962 may still be relevant today in our understanding of this complex form of trauma bonding (McLeod, 2023). They believed that there are two factors at play when understanding how emotions are formed: physiological arousal and cognitive interpretation. As discussed earlier, the moment the body senses a threat, it starts preparing to react with a heightened heart rate and muscle contraction. The brain then appraises and labels this arousal by picking up environmental cues. If a victim picks up the perceived "kindness" of the abuser, they're very likely to label their interactions with the abuser positively—maybe even romantically.

You can, therefore, see how this form of trauma bonding can be particularly relevant in relationships with parents, partners, or others whom the victim perceives to be a loved one. What the victim may not realize is that this supposedly loving relationship is characterized by a clear power imbalance (financial, social, or emotional) between themself and the abuser. Over time, this imbalance can create a strong sense of dependence on their abuser, whereby the victim constantly looks to the abuser not only for survival but also for emotional validation. This dependence can intensify further if the abuser has successfully isolated their victim and led them to believe that no help is ever going to arrive.

Apart from this power imbalance and dependence, the abuser/victim relationships in Stockholm syndrome are characterized by the victim's deep mistrust of outsiders. They may begin to distrust law enforcement, rescuers, or others who try to intervene, eventually believing the abuser's warnings that these outsiders will only make things worse as no one but the abuser cares for or understands them.

Stockholm syndrome is often a survival instinct directed solely toward self-preservation. Victims may believe that showing loyalty, gratitude, or affection to their abuser may increase the odds of their safety. Now, let's see how this ties into the cognitive dissonance we discussed earlier. Victims experience conflicting feelings about the abuser's cruelty and kindness and their own desire to stay and leave. Since they've already been conditioned to stay via the tactics of love-bombing, fear, and intimidation, the only way they can resolve their internal conflict is by modifying their feelings and beliefs. They may, thus, downplay the abuser's harmful actions and focus on the positive aspects of the relationship. In this process, they also convince themselves that the abuser is kind and gentle and that they truly love them. Why else would they stay?

The Trauma Bonding Test

While all of these concepts are interesting and easy to grasp on a theoretical level, assessing them in real life can be slightly more challenging. Here are a few statements that may help you understand if you have a trauma bond with an abuser. Again, a small reminder that this isn't a standardized test but is instead intended to give you an insight into your own psychological relationship with the abuser. Respond to each question with "never," "rarely," "sometimes," "often," or "always":

5. I feel like I'm addicted to them and, no matter how much I try to move away, I always come back.

6. Their approval means the world to me, especially after abusive episodes.

7. I try to justify or hide their temper tantrums from outsiders because I feel like they're just misunderstood by the world.

8. I engage in behaviors such as self-harm, drinking, and so on to calm the chaos and confusion within.

9. I feel deeply shameful for triggering their anger.

10. I forgive some of their behaviors, despite them being deal-breakers, because I know their heart is in the right place.

11. I think about how I can change myself and what I can do differently to please them.

12. I keep hoping that things will get better because I believe they're a genuinely kind human being.

13. I minimize their flaws and exaggerate their qualities to convince others of their kindness.

14. I try not to upset them so they aren't forced to reveal their dark side.

Introspecting over these statements may make you identify trauma bonds you never knew existed. Forgive yourself, and remember that these trauma bonds are created by years of conditioning. Therefore, it stands to reason that they can also be overcome with intention and time. The goal isn't to stop at creating awareness within but rather to heal and build a new life for yourself that you truly deserve. With an elaborate understanding of the fundamentals of abuse, now let's shift gears and begin your journey of healing and recovery.

Part II: Healing Yourself

Chapter 5:

The Before and After of a Narcissistic Relationship—Recognizing the Red Flags and the Aftermath

By now, you're well-versed in the tactics that a narcissistic abuser uses to manipulate you to get the continual supply of admiration and attention they crave. Remember that narcissistic supply is a pathway for a narcissist to feed their false self and avoid facing their true self. They thrive on people's submissiveness in relationships and, thus, are willing to do anything it takes to prevent the victim from leaving.

You're also aware of the stages of the abuse cycle—idealization, devaluing, repetition, and discarding—as we unravel the nightmare known as a narcissistic abusive relationship. It's no secret that both the beginning and end of these abusive relationships can be overwhelming, often blurring the individual's ability to think clearly. This chapter equips you with the information you need to assess your abusive relationship at different stages.

But before moving forward, let's address a concern that comes up frequently in my therapy sessions. Now that you're reading through the "Healing Yourself" part of this book, you might be wondering why we can't just move on to the recovery steps and why we're still harping on about the abuse itself. Frequently, I see my clients itching to jump into action once they understand the abusive dynamics of their relationship. However, before getting busy with recovery steps, it's critical that you understand what you're getting into (or getting out of).

The truth is that a narcissistic abuser is adept at manipulating your reality, and a detailed awareness of their tactics, red flags, and overall psyche is your best bet against that manipulation. In a nutshell, this awareness of what to expect is your first step in the healing journey.

The Before: Recognizing the Red Flags in the Dating Stage

While all of the tactics we've discussed, such as love-bombing, gaslighting, stonewalling, restrictions, and so on, are all red flags in themselves, they may not be all that visible through the rose-tinted glasses typical during the "honeymooning period" of new relationships. Therefore, it helps to take a step back from the abusive setting and identify certain broader red flags that may be your sign to stay away. I urge you to keep an eye out for these not only in your interactions with the person themself but also in their interactions with others. This is especially crucial in the love-bombing phase, when they'll be nothing less than wonderful to you but their narcissistic traits might be more obvious in their interactions with others. Paying attention to these red flags may allow you to get out of a possibly toxic relationship before things get serious:

- **Arrogance and entitlement:** One of the most obvious signs of a narcissistic person is the overflowing sense of entitlement. While at first glance the narcissist may project extreme charm as part of their confident self, the thin veneer of restraint they showed initially soon wears off. The confidence then morphs into an arrogance in which they truly believe that they *must* get everything they desire. In their view, everyone else exists only to do their bidding. Everyone, including their parents, siblings, best friends, and spouse, has one value to a narcissist: to feed their insatiable ego. Moreover, these demands are rarely reasonable, and even if others fulfill these unreasonable demands, they show no gratitude. A great setting to help you assess their behavior is a restaurant. Though they may treat you exceptionally well on the first date, pay attention to how they treat the staff. Do they treat the waiter as being beneath them, or make them uncomfortable with their sarcastic humor or snobby remarks? If the answer's yes, then it's best to turn around, walk out, and delete their number!

- **Rage episodes:** Dysregulated rage is another telltale sign that may be visible even before you get into a close relationship with a narcissist. Road rage is a classic example of these angry outbursts. Now, you may argue that considering these road rage incidents as narcissistic behaviors is a tad far-fetched. After all, road rage meltdowns may happen due to several reasons, such as drinking, stress, or someone simply having a bad day. All these are valid points—at least partially. I say "partially" because, no matter what anyone says, not everyone who's drunk, stressed, or having a bad day necessarily gets into an all-consuming rage to the point of harming someone else physically or psychologically. Of course, people get upset all the time, but dysregulated rage is so much more than that—it's screaming, throwing and kicking things, verbal threats, and sometimes even manipulative self-harm. These rage episodes should give you pause even if they happen only once. However, if they occur repeatedly, it's best to de-escalate the relationship as soon as possible.

- **Carelessness:** This may seem like a harmless personality trait, but viewing it through the lens of narcissistic abuse may offer valuable insights. I know what you're thinking: *We've all been careless at some point—for instance, I may have forgotten to RSVP to an important event or to wish a loved one "happy birthday."* However, the distinguishing factor between this kind of carelessness and narcissistic carelessness is the reason from which it stems. Most of us forget to do these things because life gets busy. However, narcissistic carelessness is often the result of thinking, *I'm too important to remember these details or consider others' feelings.* Someone who repeatedly changes or cancels plans at the last moment without any consideration for how it affects your schedule or feelings may be a red flag—they may be someone you want to stay away from. Of course, not everyone who's careless can be labeled a narcissist, but this trait, in combination with others, is a red flag you need to watch out for.

- **Lack of empathy:** We've talked about this over and over, but again, this isn't always easy to spot in your initial interactions with a narcissist. One trick to identify a lack of empathy is to observe your communication. Narcissists are most often conversation hogs who always find ways to talk about their experiences, past traumas, and future ambitions. The moment the conversation steers in your direction, they get uncomfortable and bored. Their need to be the center of attention is so intense that it frequently shows itself, even when they're trying to make you feel special.

- **Absence of meaningful long-term relationships:** This one's a definite red flag and may be obvious if you know what to look for. A narcissist may portray themself as the unlucky victim of a detached family, bad friendships, and toxic past relationships. However, this lack of close, meaningful relationships is more likely than not their own doing. One thing to understand about a narcissist's relationships is that they may have several admirers but almost no friends. This is because, although they discard people close to them, they still need acquaintances to stroke their ego in the form of validation and praise. These acquaintances are easy to keep, too, because all the narcissist has to do is project a temporary kind and charismatic image. On the other hand, maintaining a long-term, meaningful relationship is much harder as it demands reciprocity, commitment, and genuine concern for the other person, all of which the narcissist is incapable of doing.

- **Difficulty apologizing:** The last red flag is an aversion to admit mistakes. This doesn't mean that the narcissist never apologizes—but when they do, they know how to weaponize that apology, too. That's to say, their apologies are usually uttered with an ulterior motive. So, you may get an apology, but it may be so loaded with excuses that it feels less like an apology and more like a manipulative justification. Their apologies may be either vague ("I feel sorry for the way it turned out"), deflective ("You've hurt me too, you know, a lot more than I've hurt you. I'll only apologize if you do so first"), or conditional ("I'm sorry if you feel hurt by what happened, but you really don't have to make such a big deal out of this"). Essentially, they're likely to use apologies as a melodramatic tool to shift blame and further guilt you into accommodating their needs. To top it all off, they may even use these veiled apologies to prove they're so much more righteous. They might say something like, "Don't you know that I always apologize when I'm in the wrong? But you know very well that this time it isn't my fault." With the perfect balance of veiled apologies and gaslighting, they may actually make their victims question themselves.

Remember that a narcissist's red flags may manifest in many more ways beyond the ones discussed here. The point is to remind yourself to be aware of these broad signs so you can see the narcissistic patterns for what they truly are.

Minding the Overt/Covert Distinction

While we're on the topic of red flags, it's worth highlighting the distinction between overt and covert narcissists. I know we discussed this when we looked at different types of narcissists right at the beginning of the book, but the overt/covert distinction becomes all the more crucial in personal relationships. This is mainly because the red flags tend to manifest in very different ways, but the goal of manipulation remains the same.

An overt narcissist has most of the defining narcissistic traits that are generally discussed as part of narcissism. These may include (but are not limited to) the following:

- a sense of grandiosity

- controlling

- exploitative

- defensive

- arrogant

- berating

- prone to throwing tantrums

- attention-seeking

So, dating an overt narcissist may feel like you're perpetually with a know-it-all who enjoys publicly demonstrating they're better than you (even though their knowledge may be wildly inaccurate). They're also likely to draw pleasure from being difficult—they may tell you off or disagree with you only to see you flustered and faltering. Your embarrassed reactions are all they need.

Even though they're likely to get on your nerves, they're still easier to spot than covert narcissists, thanks to their desire to show off. Once you know what to look for on the narcissism checklists, their charm and confidence are usually not very challenging to recognize or resist. On the other end of the spectrum, though, are the covert narcissists, who may be a lot more difficult to spot.

A covert narcissist is likely to have all the same characteristics as the overt narcissist except the bragging displays. They choose to follow an entirely different path to achieve more or less the same objectives as an overt narcissist. In other words, while the overt narcissist is a creature who flaunts their grandiosity, the covert narcissist projects a timid, submissive image to catch your attention and sympathy. They aren't too big on gaining the approval of the masses but instead thrive on feeding off the attention of their chosen victims. This is often more harmful to the victim, because the covert narcissist's manipulative ways can destroy every last bit of the victim's resolve. Their traits may include the following:

- constant self-victimization

- blaming others

- emotional blackmail

- causing interpersonal chaos

- making up stories

- being clingy and possessive

They use these tools to create a climate of pity in the victim's mind. This sense of concern may play a critical role in the subtle gaslighting. Note that they may not gaslight you as a regular narcissist would. Instead, they may use passive-aggressive methods, such as spreading rumors and guilt-tripping, to make you doubt your reality. And, since they've created within you a sense of concern and pity for themself, you may be much more prone to believing their version rather than questioning their intentions.

An example will help you better understand the scenario. Josh decided to surprise his (covert narcissistic) girlfriend for Valentine's Day. He had a perfectly romantic night planned out, complete with flowers, dinner at her favorite restaurant, and a picnic dessert with wine at a drive-in theater. When he picked up his girlfriend and told her about the plan, she seemed a little disappointed. But Josh wasn't worried, because he was sure her mood would lift as the night progressed. He had no idea what was in store for him. Just as they sat down at their reserved table, his girlfriend started crying—very subtly at first.

When Josh asked her why, she showed him a picture of her ex, who had taken his current girlfriend on an expensive vacation. When Josh explained that he didn't have that kind of money or vacation time at work, she continued crying and saying things like, "It's not your fault; I know you don't have a high-paying job like my ex. I'll just have to make do with what I get," and "You never have time to do the things I want anyway." The night ended with Josh being disappointed in himself despite all the efforts he'd put in and his girlfriend getting all the attention and sympathy she'd wanted in the first place. As a bonus, Josh is now working extra hard to plan a vacation that will please her.

What makes these covert narcissistic patterns more dangerous is that they often aren't obvious at the beginning of a romantic relationship. It may seem as if the narcissist is simply baring their soul and being vulnerable, which intensifies the victim's attachment. It's only much later that they realize the manipulative ploy that was at work all along. That being said, paying attention to the covert narcissist's manipulative, belittling, exaggerated bids for sympathy may help you pump the brakes on the relationship in time.

Rules of Disengagement to Cope With a Narcissistic Relationship

Spotting red flags is great, but what if you're already in a relationship with a narcissist? People often ask me about the boundaries they should set with their abuser and how to put them in place. The truth is, there are no boundaries a narcissist won't cross; therefore, boundary-setting as a strategy doesn't really work. However, even though you may not be able to set boundaries *with* a narcissist, you can certainly set your boundaries *around* them. What I mean by this is that there's no point expecting a narcissist to respect your boundaries. Instead, setting the boundaries of disengagement for yourself may be much more effective.

The first thing to understand is that this kind of disengagement is impossible without radical acceptance. Radical acceptance is all about making peace with the fact that your relationship with a narcissist is *never* going to get better. Period. Most victims take a long time to get to this stage because, thanks to their abuser's breadcrumbing, they may always find themselves *hoping* for things to be better.

Take, for instance, a mother who wails in a melodramatic fashion because her daughter has chosen to go out with her friends instead of spending time with her. As the daughter starts to disengage, the mother starts behaving in a more understanding and seemingly genuine way, making the daughter believe that she can be authentic with her mother rather than disengaging from her. However, little does the daughter know that yet another episode of narcissistic rage is just around the corner—and the vicious cycle goes on and on.

Radical acceptance means setting a boundary for yourself about how engaged or disengaged you want to stay with the abuser. In Chapter 2, we briefly mentioned the technique called gray-rocking, in which you make yourself as unresponsive and uninteresting to a narcissist as possible. The idea here is for you to stop being their supply without actually ending contact with them. I also mentioned earlier that gray-rocking comes with certain caveats. It's crucial to understand these before using this powerful technique. In other words, you want to be sure what gray-rocking is and isn't (DoctorRamani, 2022):

- **Gray-rocking isn't stonewalling:** Remember how stonewalling is one of the narcissist's favorite techniques? Unfortunately, many observers, including narcissists themselves, may view gray-rocking as something similar when it's definitely not. Remember that stonewalling is an avoidance strategy whereas gray-rocking is a disengagement technique. When gray-rocking, you don't avoid or ignore any questions. Rather, you answer them factually with the least amount of emotional effect.

- **Gray-rocking isn't passive-aggressive or hostile:** When you're being showered with sly comments, condescension, or backhanded compliments, it's natural for you to want to hit back with some passive-aggressive remarks of your own. However, hostility of any kind is still engagement, and gray-rocking is all about keeping engagement as far from your interactions as possible. In fact, this lack of engagement can be particularly upsetting for the narcissist, and you can be sure that they'll come back harder with retorts that try to force you to react in some way. This is why gray-rocking can be very difficult, because you might need to keep the disengagement going even in the face of intense provocation.

- **Gray-rocking isn't giving up:** Many victims of emotional abuse know that they'll be ridiculed regardless of whether they share positive or negative news. They've come to understand that, no matter what, the abuser will invalidate their feelings and make themselves the center of the conversation. Eventually, they stop sharing anything; this often feels like a silent withdrawal and can be extremely damaging to their psyche. Many of my clients wonder how this is any different from gray-rocking. The answer lies in the intent—while the silent withdrawal happens unintentionally over time, gray-rocking is a purposeful withdrawal to prevent further emotional turmoil. Understand that the former takes power away from you whereas the latter puts you in charge, which can feel tremendously empowering.

Now for the disclaimer that I frequently remind my clients about: Though gray-rocking is a recommended strategy for dealing with narcissistic abusers, it still may not feel like a positive thing. After all, it may require you to put on a mask of nonengagement when you might really be craving some genuine exchanges. Moreover, gray-rocking an abusive partner may not be a healthy interaction for your children to witness. In cases where this extreme form of disengagement isn't possible, you might want to go with what's known as "yellow-rocking."

Yellow-rocking is especially relevant when you're co-parenting a child. Here, you replace the almost robotic responses of gray-rocking with ones that are a little more courteous, but still minus the emotion. You still consciously avoid the justifications, arguments, defensiveness, and explanations, but you do so with a slightly more animated tone. Many of my clients find this to be almost like faking niceness to their abuser. However, the truth is, you aren't doing this to be nice to the abuser but to ensure your children don't suffer the consequences of a fallout.

The After: Dealing With the Aftermath

As I've mentioned before, the best way to deal with a narcissist is not to deal with them at all. Nothing is as effective as distancing yourself from them wherever possible. But as necessary as this is, it can also feel absolutely life-shattering, at least in the moment that it happens.

There are two ways in which a breakup with a narcissist can go down—either they discard you because you're no longer offering them their narcissistic supply, or you decide to end the relationship. Remember that in an intimate relationship, the abusive partner *will not leave you* unless they've secured another source of narcissistic supply. In this case, they'll ruthlessly flaunt their new supply in front of you with no consideration for your feelings. Even though the person you loved (or still love) replacing you hurts a great deal, it may still offer you a somewhat clean way out of this messy relationship. On the other hand, if you choose to walk out, the narcissist will most definitely make your life infinitely difficult with their post-breakup tactics.

Sure, no breakups are easy, but breaking up with a narcissistic abuser can be a lot messier than usual. The abuser's impact on your life may be so traumatizing that, even after you leave, you may be haunted by regret and what you may remember as good memories. I know it seems like a "damned if you do and damned if you don't" kind of a catch-22 situation. But the reality (that your abuser doesn't wish you to know) is that once the storm calms down, breaking out of this abusive relationship will feel like the best decision of your life. However, getting to the stage where you can appreciate your decision to leave may indeed prove to be a trial by fire, thanks to certain peculiar patterns of the narcissist:

- **Hoovering:** Hoovering is often used as a synonym for vacuuming and, just as a vacuum cleaner sucks in the dust, a narcissist will try everything in their power to suck you back into their life. Hoovering is designed to leverage your insecurities in the abuser's favor. For instance, if you feel guilty for leaving, the abuser may say something like, "You can't do this to me now. I'll have nothing to live for if you leave." If the abuser senses that you miss them, they might say, "I miss you so much. I can't live without you; please come back." If they know that anger is dominating your emotions, they may say, "You were right to leave me; I never treated you right. If you give me one last chance, I'll be better—I promise."

  You can see how cleverly they mold their words to fit different situations. If only they meant what they said. To some extent, their claims about missing you or not having anything worthwhile in their life may even be true, but not in the way you hope for. For them, it all comes down to losing their supply—something they have difficulty dealing with.

- **Future-faking:** Think of this as a combination of love-bombing and hoovering. While hoovering plays on the victim's insecurities, future-faking caters to their hopes. When the narcissist sees you leaving, they'll promise you the moon and the stars. They'll show you a future where both of you have the life you've always dreamed of.

Let's say a couple differs in their desire to have children. The wife really wants them while the narcissistic husband doesn't. Now, such differences may occur even in healthy relationships. Even though it might hurt, both individuals may realize that these differences cannot be overcome and either come to a compromise or part ways. In a narcissistic relationship, however, the husband may say that he isn't ready to be a father now but will get there in a couple of years once his career takes off. The wife, thanks to her trusting nature, may agree to wait.

The problem comes when, even after two years, the husband keeps making excuses for not having kids. It's only after a bunch of these never-ending excuses that the wife realizes it's never going to happen. You need to understand that the husband doesn't delay this because he isn't sure. Rather, he's absolutely certain he never wanted kids to begin with, yet he keeps stringing his wife along simply because he doesn't want to lose his supply. Sharing the limelight with a new little bundle of joy just doesn't fit into his plan; he's the only star allowed in his wife's life. I know a husband who actually told his wife that he started to lose feelings for her when she had their first child. As a mother, she didn't appear to be all his. He felt slighted at every turn because he now had to share her and her time with their new baby.

The trick that the narcissist employs here is that the future-faking is always believable, which keeps you stuck. Your mind may engage in the cognitive bias called "sunk-cost fallacy," where you feel like all the time and effort you put into this relationship will be wasted if you leave now. If you've already waited for two years, what's a few more months? And so you wait for a future that's never going to be a reality.

- **Smear campaigns:** When the narcissist realizes they can't get you back through their charming sweet talk, they bring out the big guns. They hate to see you leaving their tightly controlled ship, so they may try to take back some control by tarnishing your character. They'll spread outrageous lies and exaggerations about you to mutual friends, family, or colleagues. These smear campaigns are frequently intended not only to undermine your credibility as an individual but also to portray themself as the poor victim who's been left stranded by you.

These smear campaigns may appear differently depending on the setting of the relationship. An abusive boss may make insulting and inaccurate remarks in your performance review while also spreading rumors about your incompetence in the workplace. A narcissistic partner may misrepresent your social drinking to be a grave substance abuse concern to prove that you're unfit to receive child custody in the divorce. Mind you, the goal isn't the welfare of the children here; the narcissist may not even want custody, but they'll fight for it with all their might just to ensure you don't get it. A narcissistic parent may tell any family members who'll listen that you abandoned them in their old age because of financial issues. These accusations become especially traumatizing as you're already trying to pick up the pieces of yourself after an emotionally difficult separation from the abuse. That's the exact aim of the attack on your character—to emotionally abuse you further out of spite and a desire for revenge.

In addition to the above, you need to consider your physical safety, because leaving a narcissist is like turning your back on a wounded lion—you never know when they'll strike back. One of my clients literally paid two guys, one of whom was armed, to keep watch while she packed and left her abuser's home. The considerations of physical and financial safety make this already excruciating choice much, much harder. In these cases, you must reach out to domestic abuse support organizations to ensure the leaving part goes smoothly. This is why awareness of what to expect and appropriate planning become the make-or-break aspects of leaving an abusive relationship. Now that we have the awareness part covered, let's move on to the step-by-step planning that allows you to break the cycle and step out of the abusive situation.

Chapter 6:

The Light of Freedom

I've said this several times before and I'll say it several times more: Leaving an abusive relationship isn't easy. You don't just wake up one day and bid farewell to the abuser. An outsider who urges you to leave may have the best of intentions, but they rarely understand the complexities of walking out of an abusive environment. Before we go into these complexities, I'd like to address the other side of the coin—staying in an abusive relationship.

Though I strongly recommend getting out of a narcissistic relationship, we must acknowledge that this is a massive step. As many benefits as it has, it also comes with certain risks. Leaving without understanding these risks is like stepping into a landmine field wearing a blindfold. Of course, these risks cannot be condensed into a template and are unique to your own situation. For example, a woman with children who has no job and no social support may have a long way to go before actually stepping out of the relationship. The situation becomes a lot more complicated when these financial concerns are entwined with verbal threats that endanger your physical safety.

If you are or have ever been in a narcissistic relationship, you'll know that a narcissist is nothing if not persistent. They'll try all the mind games to get you back—and when they fail, their vengeance may not know any bounds. This is why preparing for the worst possible scenario is critical. At this preparation stage, you're the best judge of what's currently possible for you and what isn't. Remember that these considerations become even more crucial when it's a relationship with an abusive intimate partner.

Before you get going with your exit plan, it's imperative that you know your *why*. Why do you wish to leave—or why do you need to stay, at least for the moment? Being clear on this why can be greatly empowering in itself. Your why is what will get you through the bad days. Before delving into this chapter, I urge you to take a moment and think about this why. Once you have it, the step-by-step plan discussed in this chapter will make a lot more sense.

A Step-By-Step Guide to Breaking the Trauma Bond

Remember the trauma bond we discussed in Chapter 4? Even before you free yourself from your abuser, you must free yourself from the trauma bond that keeps you stuck in the situation. Since trauma bonding is quite an overwhelming topic for most, let's break it down into clear, actionable steps.

Step 1: Acknowledge the Abuse

As in Katherine's case from the Introduction, most people have a really hard time naming problematic patterns as abuse. To them, abuse seems like an exaggerated word when, in reality, their lived experience is nothing short of abuse. A large part of this may come from cultural conditioning, as acknowledging abuse for what it is may be considered "washing your dirty linen in public" in many societies.

Even when they come into therapy, these abused victims often say things like, "I just don't understand what I'm doing wrong!" When I use the term "abuse" for their experience, they interject, sometimes vehemently, explaining why it's not abuse:

- "Abuse is too extreme; he's never been violent or aggressive with me."

- "Abuse makes it sound so much worse than it is!"

- "You can't say this is abuse—all relationships have their issues, after all."

- "He has his quirks, but he would never do anything to hurt me intentionally, let alone abuse me!"

This, then, leads to the classic trauma bonding pattern of making excuses for the abuser, which further strengthens the trauma bond. Therefore, the first step is to acknowledge the abuse.

This may seem simple enough on paper, but it can be tremendously difficult for the victims. This is because the abuse often leads them to a point where they just cannot trust their feelings and thoughts. If you can't trust what you're feeling, how do you conclude you're being abused? How can you be certain that you aren't the narcissistic abuser yourself? Well, there are two simple ways of doing this. First is that if you're doubting yourself and wondering if you're the abuser, then you most likely aren't. Narcissistic abusers don't really get into that kind of introspective space.

The second test is one that's recommended by Dr. Ramani Durvasula and is a little more concrete (Pau, 2024). When you start doubting your thoughts and feelings, pay attention to your energy levels. Do you feel completely drained after spending time with this person? If yes, then it's likely because you're always walking on eggshells and your brain is constantly calculating the best way to respond without causing any drama.

I had a client who went through a similar difficult phase where she just couldn't accept that her husband was being abusive. But as we went through therapy, she realized the amount of stress she was under when interacting with her husband. In one of the later sessions, she said, "Things seemed so easy when he wasn't around and I wasn't watching my every move. Even my interactions with the kids felt so much more fulfilling." Acknowledgment of the abuse is the first step toward that kind of fulfillment.

Step 2: Examine Your Own Early Attachment Patterns

The victim's childhood trauma may attract narcissistic relationships later in life, especially because the narcissist knows the best way to exploit that trauma to their advantage. Now, this is in no way meant to blame the victim or to state that the responsibility for abuse lies with the victim. Absolutely not. However, the victim's unfulfilled desire to overcome their childhood insecurities frequently becomes an obstacle to leaving an abusive relationship. It's almost as if the victim tries over and over to make right those things they were powerless to address as a child.

Take, for example, Caleb's narcissistic mother, who was distant for the most part but would breadcrumb him when she needed validation. Thanks to this unpredictable attachment behavior, Caleb grew utterly unsure of his own thoughts and feelings. After two failed long-term romantic relationships, he lost all confidence and started using humor to deflect focus from his insecurities by calling himself the "disaster magnet." Only after he entered therapy was he able to draw parallels between his adult relationships and his dysfunctional relationship with his mother. As he sat on the couch in front of me during one session, he had a moment of revelation, realizing he was always getting into relationships with women who had the same emotionally unavailable and manipulative traits that his mother exhibited. And no matter how much he tried to stay firm about his needs, he would always end up chasing his partners. He'd almost beg for their attention, affection, and validation, which never really came. To top it all off, he'd end up validating their feelings whenever they chose to grace him with their emotional presence.

Unless and until you take a step back and work on these patterns, hopefully with professional therapy, you'll likely keep reinforcing the existing trauma bond unknowingly. You may even find yourself repeatedly attracted to similar narcissistic personalities.

Step 3: Evaluate the Relationship Mindfully

Whether it's love-bombing, hoovering, or future-faking, a narcissistic abuser's lies are always future-oriented. They manipulate you into visualizing a grand future, which may be the very thing you desire for the two of you. Unfortunately, this future never becomes a reality. Your trauma bond with the abuser may push you to give them infinite second chances while also justifying their actions:

- "He's right, you know—he doesn't have the time to think of a baby right now."

- "He had the best business plan when he borrowed money from me, but the economy has just been very difficult. He'll return it soon."

- "She's promised that she'll sort through our relationship issues once I move to a different city with her. She just thinks we need a fresh start. She'll go for therapy as soon as we settle into the new place."

When dealing with a narcissist, it's important to be mindful of the relationship as it is in the present moment. Note that narcissistic abusers rarely change substantially enough to make things better. They might put on a performative act temporarily, but in the long run they often revert to their abusive patterns. Thinking of the relationship in the *now* can help jolt you awake from the false dreams the narcissist is showing you to keep you around.

Step 4: Specify the Abuse

As you begin looking at the relationship through a realistic, present-oriented lens, the abuse might become much clearer. In an abusive relationship, the abuser will constantly give you reasons to be with them. This, combined with your own desire to make the relationship work, only strengthens the existing trauma bond, making it more and more challenging to leave. Since the abuser gives you multiple pros (which are mostly inaccurate and exaggerated), it's up to you to make a relationship cons list for yourself.

Before you do that, however, let's address a common question that many of my clients ask me: How do you differentiate between narcissistic abuse and issues that all couples face? Well, anyone who's been in any kind of relationship knows that all relationships can get messy. Even a healthy relationship between two relatively emotionally unscathed people can run into bumps centered around financial issues, work–life balance, contribution to household chores, and so on. However, the one factor that can transform these scenarios into emotionally abusive situations is the uncertainty typical of a narcissistic relationship. For instance, in a healthy relationship, the two partners may scream at each other and even fling deep insults at each other.

However, at no point will one partner gaslight the other into making them feel like they're crazy. In an abusive relationship, the sense of confusion is always present, even when the two parties aren't arguing.

With that distinction in mind, try to note down all the times this relationship has made you feel distinctly uncomfortable. By this, I don't just mean the berating and ridicule during arguments but also in your daily life.

Step 5: Seek Professional Help

Having a narcissist distort your entire sense of reality often makes you feel like your life is blowing up in a different way every day. Going through this consistently can significantly deplete your mental resources. This is why you may not be left with much fuel in the tank when it comes to getting out of the relationship. Therefore, no matter how strong your resolve, it's always recommended that you work with a certified therapist in your healing journey.

Furthermore, even as you decide to end the abusive relationship, you may struggle with intense guilt. This is because many narcissistic abusers are negatively impacted when their victims leave. This may be because they lose their narcissistic supply, but can also be because they depend on their victim to complete various chores. For instance, an abusive husband may rely on his wife completely for his meals. When a victim sees the negative impact they've created for their abuser, they frequently start exhibiting physical symptoms themself. So, when a wife leaves and sees the physical toll it's taken on her abusive husband, she herself may lose sleep and appetite. It's important to understand that these physical symptoms may also have their roots in the trauma bond. Having a professional by your side as you resolve these physical and emotional entanglements is a very helpful, if not necessary, asset.

You must keep in mind one crucial point in this regard: Choose a therapist who has experience in dealing with narcissistic abuse. I can't tell you how many times clients have come to me saying their previous therapy attempts only made things worse. This isn't to blame anyone or criticize any style of therapy, but we must acknowledge that narcissistic abuse is not the same as other issues.

Here's a common example of this distinction: When healthy couples encounter difficult situations, it may be easy to identify communication as a commonplace issue. This means that when the therapist helps the couple work on their communication patterns and styles, there may well be considerable improvement. However, the same cannot be said of a narcissistic relationship. Telling the abused partner to simply try to talk to the narcissistic abuser may—and most likely will—invite, if not create, more issues for the individual, making the abuse even worse.

Therefore, it's critical that you work with a therapist who's aware of these abusive patterns and of the appropriate ways of dealing with them to avoid exacerbating the abuse. The therapist may also need to be mindful of not triggering the narcissist to the extent that they cancel therapy altogether and even forbid the victim to attend therapy sessions. Besides therapy, joining support groups can also prove to be helpful. Connecting with others who have experienced similar abuse can be incredibly validating and healing.

Leaving the Abuser Behind

The complicated nature of abusive relationships means that the end of a relationship can come about in many different ways. Here, I'm not talking about who ends the relationship but how it's ended. Needless to say, not all of these ways are necessarily healthy. Let's look at the most common ways in which a victim may choose to leave their abuser behind and the pros and cons of each (DoctorRamani, 2024):

- **No contact:** This is the most obvious way, where you cut ties completely and do everything possible to avoid interacting with the abuser ever again. Victims who adopt a no-contact approach may withdraw completely from any mutual social circles and may even resort to restraining orders to keep their abuser away. While it absolutely works, it may not always be possible for everyone. For example, it may be possible in a group of friends but not when two partners share custody of a child. Even for those for whom it's possible, it can be a very difficult decision as it may require you to leave behind a big chunk of your social circle alongside your abuser, which may include mutual friends and even in-laws who've come to be close to you. If you're going no-contact, you must be emotionally prepared to be judged and blamed for ending the relationship, not just by your abuser but also by people you value.

- **Low contact:** Most people prefer to have a low-contact policy. This means that, though the relationship has ended, they still have some contact with their abuser. The gray-rocking and yellow-rocking we discussed in Chapter 5 are a part of this. Going low contact is often the most positively perceived way of ending an abusive relationship, especially by mutual social circles and even the courts in the case of a custody battle. That being said, this can prove to be quite challenging for those who carry deep wounds from the abuse. Facing your abuser and resisting the urge to fall into their traps is no easy feat and may require a great deal of practice to master.

- **Geographical separation:** The last method of leaving an abusive relationship is simply moving away from the abuser. This doesn't really apply to romantic partners but may be more common if the issue is toxic family and friends. Take, for instance, moving out of your parents' home and, consequently, away from a narcissistic parent. This can seem deceptively simple and effective, but, in reality, the distance may not be the antidote you hope for. For most people, trauma follows them wherever they go. Overcoming this trauma may become even more difficult without a sense of closure, as they never ended the relationship formally. In these situations, the use of radical acceptance, which we spoke about in Chapter 5, is paramount. Without this acceptance, the abusive patterns you encounter occasionally in family gatherings or even in text groups can catch you off guard quite easily.

As you become aware of these intricacies, you'll realize that ending an abusive relationship isn't just about staying or leaving the abuser's immediate physical vicinity; it's also about taking the time to consciously set disengagement boundaries for yourself.

Figuring Out the Technicalities

While the emotional details are critical, having your logistics planned out is just as important when ending an abusive relationship. In this section, we'll discuss three facets of ending the relationship that require careful consideration.

Creating a Safety Plan

If you're considering leaving an abuser, a safe exit plan is one of the first things to think about. As mentioned before, you can't just up and leave an abusive relationship. Without the right kind of planning, several aspects may go terribly wrong, endangering you and your loved ones even further. Here are a few things you must keep in mind when deciding how and when to leave. These are especially crucial if your abuser has a past history of physical abuse or even extreme rage that may not have *yet* slipped into violent aggression:

- **Safe places in the house:** If you don't yet have a definite plan for leaving, a good place to start is by identifying the safe places in the house. This would include rooms that have no weapons or other objects that could be used as weapons, and that have an emergency exit such as a door or window. Most often, kitchens, bathrooms, and stairs pose added dangers in escalated situations, so try to stay clear of them when possible. You might also want to avoid wearing clothing and accessories that may be used as a weapon against you, such as scarves or necklaces that could be used as a strangling tool.

- **Transportation:** Having some form of transportation out of an abusive situation will prove extremely useful if things escalate unexpectedly. If you can, try to keep a set of car keys where your abuser isn't able to access them. This is essential, because abusers often snatch their victim's keys in an attempt to keep them from leaving. It's also a great habit to ensure that your car is fueled up and in good condition at all times.

- **Seeking support:** One of the first things you want to do is identify some trusted people. This may be a neighbor, a family member, or a friend. If open communication with them isn't possible in an escalated situation, make sure you have a signal that tells them you need help. This may be anything from closing a specific window shade to turning on the porch light. With this signal, they then know to help by taking the children temporarily or calling the authorities. If your children are old enough, you can even teach them how to call 911 and get help.

- **Essentials for the exit:** Make sure you have an "essentials bag" ready to go. You may want to stash away some cash, your legal documents, clothing, and other essentials such as medicines or diapers. Taking credit cards may be risky, because the location of each transaction is easy to track down, giving your abuser your exact location. Legal documents such as passports, birth certificates, citizenship documents, educational certificates, your marriage certificate, and so on are an absolutely necessity.

- **Safety after leaving:** Most victims are so overwhelmed by the logistical details of leaving the abusive situation that they simply cannot imagine anything beyond that point. The truth is, leaving is just one part of getting out of an abusive relationship. Keeping yourself and your children (if you have them with you) safe after you leave is just as important. This is why you must consider how accessible you wish to be through phone, email, and social media after you leave. Getting a new telephone number and disabling your social media accounts for a while might be advisable, depending on your situation.

Whenever I discuss these measures with my clients who are thinking of leaving, I receive a common response: "All of these seem pretty intense and more geared toward physical abuse. My partner would never go that far." To some extent, they're right, in that a safety plan is made while keeping in mind the physical safety of an individual. However, it's also important to remember that when an emotional abuser knows you're trying to leave, the situation may escalate much more quickly and unexpectedly than you could ever imagine. It's always better to have these safety measures in place and never use them than to regret not having them ready and at hand when you do need them.

Dealing With Post-Separation Abuse

In the previous chapter, we spoke about three patterns—hoovering, future-faking, and smear campaigns—that are characteristic of the aftermath of narcissistic abuse. It's important to remember, however, that these may not necessarily endanger your physical safety. If you can white-knuckle your way through the emotional mind games, you might be able to cope with the trauma over time. However, post-separation abuse may take a much darker and more dangerous turn. The abuser, in these cases, may resort to one of the following tactics:

- **Stalking and harassment:** Relentless calls, texts, and emails may be just the beginning of their attempts to harass you. After the relationship has ended, the messages may not even be directed at getting you back but may rather take the shape of vengeful rants about how you deserve all the worst things in life. They could even take the harassment further, extending it to stalking and monitoring you, your new life, your activities, and even your new location with or without your knowledge. It's not uncommon for abusers to put trackers on the vehicles of their victims. In addition to being incredibly traumatizing, this type of harassment also puts the victim and their loved ones in very real physical danger.

- **False legal allegations:** Many narcissistic abusers use the judicial system to do their dirty work for them. They may make false claims of criminal behavior on your part or accuse you of child abuse or neglect.

  I remember one of my clients who walked into our session completely defeated and clueless about what to do. She mentioned how she and her family had just moved to a new neighborhood and her husband had had a difference of opinion with the homeowner association (HOA) president in an HOA meeting. Though the husband had followed all the rules and regulations, the person with whom he'd argued was so offended by the challenge to her authority that she went on to make life hell for my client's family. Though my client could never prove it, she and her husband had to face a barrage of police inquiries all of a sudden, from allegations of drunk driving to not feeding their children.

Of course, nothing ever came of these claims because they were never founded on any facts, but it got to the point where my client and her husband had no clue as to when they would be stopped and interrogated. Moreover, the initial shock of the inquiries was so intense that they never had the time to consider who could have made these false reports. After all, thinking someone is purposely targeting you, trying to discredit you with false legal allegations just to harass you, isn't the first explanation most of us would come to. My client and her husband assumed these were just misunderstandings. It was only later, when the woman made a peculiar remark, that they traced this malicious reporting back to her.

Remember, the lady's goal was probably never to get them arrested—she was smart enough to know that her claims wouldn't hold up under scrutiny. Instead, her ultimate goal was vengeful in nature and was designed to disturb her targets' mental peace and keep them tangled up in legal hassles.

Such legal allegations may become significantly worse when leveled by an intimate partner. In these scenarios, the abuser may even make claims that are harder to verify—such as allegations of parental alienation, where they claim you've purposefully kept them away from their children or have damaged their relationship with the children in some way. This is particularly frustrating when the abuser is the one trying their best to alienate the children from you. The point is that the abuser can keep you entangled in these impossible litigations. Seeing you frustrated and having to be in constant touch with them when you were trying to escape fulfills their goal of holding on to you, along with preventing you from moving on without them.

- **Financial entrapment:** Financial dependence on the abuser is one of the most common reasons for victims to feel stuck in their abusive situations. Remember that this financial dependence doesn't just happen but is very well designed by the abuser. Often, they'll have crippled their victim's finances so badly that the victim can't even imagine leaving. This financial dependence may continue even after the separation, and the abuser could certainly exploit it to assert their dominance. This exploitation may be obvious in some cases—refusing to pay court-ordered alimony and common bills such as children's school fees, or refusing to honor mutual debts, for instance—or it may be sneakier, such as using your credit card without your knowledge or claiming to lose or break essentials that you'll have no choice but to replace. If you can swallow the financial loss, it's best to just move on without resorting to arguments and fights. Unfortunately, however, that's not a luxury most victims can afford. So, the emotional abuse may continue to a large extent with the added burden of financial troubles.

- **Coercion and intimidation:** Again, coercion may be obvious, as in the case of threats, breaking objects, or damaging your property, but it can also be much more indirect, such as threatening someone else who crosses their path to show you what they're capable of or displaying weapons in front of you. If children are involved, the abuser may also threaten to keep you from seeing them post-separation. They may even threaten to hurt themself to assert their control over you.

Remember that the goal of discussing these forms of post-separation abuse is not to scare you into staying. I've worked with several abuse victims over the years, and the great majority of them recount the immediate period after separation as one of the most difficult times of their lives. However, not a single client of mine has ever expressed that they wish they'd just stayed with their abuser.

Exposing the Lies and the Liar

After everything a narcissistic abuser has put you through, it's natural for you to want to burst out the speakers and tell the world about the horrible person they are. Unfortunately, however, this may not be as straightforward as you hope. One of my clients came to understand this the hard way when he stood up for himself by trying to expose his boss's manipulative tactics, only to be labeled as the manipulative one himself by the entire department.

In short, exposing the narcissist comes with considerable risk. For someone who values their public perception so deeply, a narcissist certainly won't take all the exposing lying down. You can be sure that they'll lash out with all the ammunition they've gathered against you in the years you've known them. As mentioned above, they'll push back by creating financial troubles or intensifying their smear campaigns, and they may even come out swinging with disturbing threats against you and your loved ones.

It's likely that you'll end up losing a lot more mental peace and even financial stability in the process of exposing their lies. Essentially, it comes down to how far you're willing to go. How much risk, if any, do you think it's worth? The wise old George Bernard Shaw quote comes to mind here: "Never wrestle with pigs. You both get dirty and the pig likes it" (Shaw, n.d.). Since the narcissist thrives on provoking a reaction from you, this kind of mental battle probably feels rewarding to them. This is why many survivors of abuse come to believe that when it comes to narcissists, the only winning move is not playing their game at all.

Don't misunderstand me, though; I'm not here to discourage you from exposing an abuser. Not at all. That's a decision only you can make. Just remember that it might come at a cost. You must know exactly what to expect before you get into it. If you know you're fighting a rattlesnake, you risk getting bitten. If you know you're engaging with a potentially lethal enemy, you know you could be harmed. Even though you may have lived with your abuser for years, you don't share their mindset. Therefore, you don't know what their reaction to what you do might be. Whatever you do is a calculated risk. Also, there's no formula or template for the perfect exposure. You need to decide what it looks like for you, and that's all that matters. For example, you might not need to tell the whole world your truth—just making sure the people you love know your side of the story might bring you all the closure you need.

Regardless of your choice regarding exposing the narcissistic abuser, it's important to document the abuse as it happens. While it's much easier to gather evidence of and prove physical abuse, emotional abuse may not always be as black-and-white. It's essential that you keep any threatening emails, texts, and voicemails you've received from the abuser. This becomes particularly crucial if you might need to pursue legal action, such as in the case of a divorce and/or a custody battle. If you've had prior legal counsel, you may even be advised to record any belittling conversations you have with your abuser. As sneaky as it may seem, it might be a necessary step on the legal road that lies ahead of you. Of course, you want to make sure you have competent professional help when considering your legal options.

Even though it may seem impossible at this point, the above-discussed aftermath of leaving the abusive relationship will settle. Eventually, it may even seem like a tiny speck (not an insignificant one—never an insignificant one, but tiny nonetheless) in the skies of your individual growth. In the next chapter, we'll explore the healing adventure that awaits you as you step into the beginning of your new life.

Chapter 7:

The Adventure Called Growth

Have you ever heard of a Japanese art form known as *kintsugi*? In this centuries-old artistic tradition, broken objects are mended with gold. As beautiful as the outcome turns out to be, this tradition is about more than simply increasing the aesthetic value of the objects. Rather, it's the broader philosophy of acknowledging the beauty of imperfections in life. When we embrace these imperfect moments with love, instead of wallowing in them or hiding them, we're bound to create something truly beautiful.

Victims of abuse often may wonder, *Why me?* And it's absolutely natural to do so. But when the dust settles and you start gaining a grip on your reality, you'll realize the bigger truth: While your life seems to be shattered into a million pieces right now, it also means you get to rebuild it from scratch with the pieces you choose for yourself. Mend it with self-love and the outcome will be nothing short of a *kintsugi* masterpiece—a testament to embracing imperfection, healing your wounds, and creating the beauty of resilience. This chapter explores the process of recovery from the trauma of abuse and the healing that ensues once you leave an abusive relationship.

From Victim to Victor

Anyone who's survived emotional abuse is undoubtedly a winner, regardless of whether they decide to stay or leave. As heartbreaking as working with emotional abuse survivors is, it's many more times inspiring. I can't tell you how often I've witnessed victims rising beautifully and graciously, much like a phoenix, from the ashes of lives in which abuse was all they'd ever known. The lives they go on to build are then founded on a strong sense of their authentic selves, which they'd been forced to hide all along.

Before going any further, I want you to take a moment to do a small exercise. Make sure you're alone in a quiet space. Below is a short list of strengths that I see flourishing in my clients all the time. Now, I want you to look at this list and put a checkmark against the strengths you believe you've gained through your extended encounter with your abuser. Feel these strengths within yourself as vividly as possible. This means I want you to think about an instance where you displayed that strength in the abusive relationship and also how that strength could help you in your new life. Here's the list:

- resilience

- greater self-awareness

- greater courage to be your authentic self

- patience

- a more effective lie-detecting radar

- a sharper gut instinct

- empathy

These are only a few strengths, so go ahead and add to them to make your own list. Remember that this exercise isn't intended to force you to find a silver lining to the horrific experience you've had. The idea isn't to get into a toxic positivity loop, where you feel the same need to fake happiness that you did with your abuser to "fit in" or be liked, injuring yourself emotionally in the process. Instead, I want you to look at the abuse experience for what it is—that's the only way to heal from the trauma. Acknowledge that enduring abusive treatment has to have changed you on the inside. When you begin to see how you've adapted to accommodate the abuse—perhaps you've stopped trusting others, stopped believing in your own worth, or bent over backward to please others—you get a sense of how being with a narcissistic abuser has changed your core beliefs about yourself and others. Only when you acknowledge and accept these changes can your path to recovery become a reality. That said, it's important to remember that recovery and healing don't happen overnight. It's a long road and you must take it at your own pace.

Phases of Recovery

After leaving their abusive relationship, many victims believe that the hard part is over and that their life will now be better almost in the blink of an eye. They're then so shocked by the bumpy road ahead of them that it almost feels like whiplash. It's important to remember that healing from trauma can take months, or sometimes even years. While it may feel like an uphill climb at times to the beautiful view from the top, the journey itself can teach you a lot about yourself. Many people will tell you to just leave it all behind and move on already, but they aren't the ones who lived with a narcissistic abuser. Even if they say they did, they didn't live with the same person you did. Other people simply don't know or understand what your life behind closed doors was like. It's of the utmost importance not to judge yourself. There's no set schedule for recovery. Remember that only you get to decide how fast or slowly you want to do this.

Dr. Judith Herman proposed that this journey is a three-step process (Larsen, 2024). Though this model was developed for trauma therapy, and the steps are best done with the help of a therapist, it provides valuable insight into the process of recovery itself.

Phase 1: Stabilization and Safety

This is the period that comes immediately after you've left the abusive situation. As you're settling into your new life, it's important to take a step back and acknowledge the terrifying roller coaster you've been on, not only in terms of the abuse but also in terms of the leaving process. Therefore, the first phase of recovery will be to stabilize these emotions while you continue to establish safety.

Remember that this safety isn't limited to physical aspects but also includes emotional safety. When you were in the abusive relationship, you may have never felt safe enough to express your true emotions. The habit of suppressing emotions may very well continue even after you break free of the abuse. This first phase is about realizing it's possible to express your emotions, both positive and negative, in a regulated manner.

Educating yourself about the abuser's patterns is often a way to undo at least some of the negative effects of abuse that you've endured. Some people may tell you that you mustn't hark back to the past and just need to move on. But making sense of your experience is critical to your healing journey, and understanding these abuse patterns may be an extremely effective means of stabilizing your emotions.

Phase 2: Remembrance and Mourning

Many abuse victims hit the ground running after they leave the abusive relationship. They're so focused on getting their life back to normal that they never get the chance to grieve the demise of the relationship. When I mention this to my clients, many of them retort with an immediate, "I'm happy I'm out; I don't need to grieve." I then remind them that this isn't necessarily about grieving their relationship with the abuser, although that might be an absolutely valid response for many victims as they may still miss or love the abuser.

But one thing that's common to all survivors is the need to grieve the loss of their relationship as an important part of their life. This includes the hopes and dreams that you once associated with the relationship. Furthermore, as mentioned earlier, abuse changes the individual in permanent ways. You likely won't be the same person you were at the beginning of the abusive relationship. The abuse may have scraped off, or at least suppressed, some aspects of your old self, and grieving those parts is crucial to the journey ahead. Because of this mourning space you give yourself, this stage is also known as the trauma processing phase.

Phase 3: Reconnection and Integration

It's only in the third phase of recovery that you might experience some sense of normalcy returning to your life. By now, you've had time to assess the impact, both short-term and long-term, that the abusive experience has had on your physical and emotional health. However, you also realize that, as significant as this experience was, it no longer has to be the defining aspect of your entire life. Now's the time to start rebuilding your life and yourself, one step at a time. This may involve building new meaningful relationships, finding a purpose that helps you heal further, and redefining your future with new goals and ambitions.

I highly recommend working through these stages under the guidance of a professional therapist who understands the dynamics of narcissism and trauma. Remember that having a comfortable rapport with your therapist is of the utmost importance. You don't have to keep powering through in a therapeutic setting that makes you uncomfortable or isn't in keeping with your own pace. Finding the right therapist for you may take some work initially, but once you find that person, the process of recovery becomes much less confusing.

Recovery Through the Lens of Therapy

While finding the right therapeutic fit is essential for virtually any psychological concern, it becomes particularly crucial in the context of recovery from narcissistic abuse. This is because narcissistic abuse is a relatively newer therapy niche and there isn't enough research or an established therapy module to rely on. Therefore, the therapeutic approach must draw from various schools of thought. This also means that a therapist may not advertise themself as a specialist in abuse recovery but may still have a helpful outlook. At the same time, someone who claims to be an expert may not always understand narcissistic dynamics. It often helps to familiarize yourself with some core therapeutic modalities.

Cognitive Behavioral Therapy

Cognitive behavioral therapy (CBT) is a popular choice when it comes to therapeutic intervention for narcissistic abuse. This therapy is too elaborate to be discussed in detail here. Therefore, let's outline the major highlights as they relate to the context of recovery from narcissistic abuse. Remember that this behavior modification approach may be counterproductive when the victim actually has an actively interactive relationship with the abuser. This is because the goal isn't to encourage the victim to modify their behavior to better adapt to the abusive environment. However, once that situation is left behind, the victim may benefit a great deal from the perspective that CBT brings.

CBT explores the circular relationship between thoughts, emotions, and feelings. It may be particularly effective in dealing with the intense shame, guilt, and self-doubt that accompany post-abuse healing. Let's take a look at the renowned ABC model in the context of the following example.

While shopping for groceries, you run into an old acquaintance who asks you about your partner. When you tell them that you're no longer together, they make a passing remark about how you were the perfect couple. On your way back home, you can't stop thinking about how you and your partner really did have great moments—how they showered you with love and gifts, and how they always said that they'd never be able to live without you. This euphoric memory intensifies the feeling that you've ruined the best thing that ever happened in your life. Then your ex leaves you one of their hoovering texts, which melts away your resolve to start anew, and, before you can blink, you're back to the life that you'd tried so hard to escape.

Now, imagine if you had a cheat sheet to warn you of such triggers in advance and prepare you to deal with the guilt and shame-inducing thoughts in a more productive way. That's exactly what the ABC model does. It allows you to identify and list all the triggers you can think of so you aren't completely overwhelmed when you encounter them. This awareness proves extremely valuable when irrational guilt and shame threaten to take over your ration brain.

The ABC model in this case would look something like this:

Antecedents	Behaviors	Consequences
This refers to the internal thoughts or external actions that lead you to a particular behavior.	This refers to the so-called problem behavior that's being assessed and what happens when the behavior is in motion.	This is what follows the behavior, both desirable and undesirable.
In this case, it's both external (accidentally meeting the acquaintance) and	Here, it could be falling for your ex's	In our example, it would include all the same old psychological distress that follows as both of you settle back into your

internal (guilt and shame).	attempts to get you back.	routines.

Being aware of these patterns of before, during, and after allows survivors to keep the overwhelm at bay, at least to some extent. When you've already gone over these ABCs in your mind, you're likely to be much better prepared to make appropriate choices when faced with these situations.

Rational Emotive Behavior Therapy

Most people assume that an event is what causes them distress. However, the rational emotive behavior therapy (REBT) school of thought begs to disagree. It emphasizes the role of our beliefs about an event, which lead to our emotional reactions. These beliefs, thoughts, and assumptions are referred to as self-talk—the raw and uncensored internal dialogue that all of us engage in. It proposes the ABCDE model, which is slightly different from the ABC model above. Let's take the same example as above to see how this model works:

Activating event	Beliefs	Consequences	Disputation	Effective new beliefs
An activating event is similar to an antecedent, as this is what triggers a particular response. The activating	These beliefs (aka self-talk) may be shaped by our early social conditioning, our own experiences, and even our observation of our surroundings. They may be rational or	The beliefs kick off a cycle of actions and emotions, which may be either positive or negative. The negative consequence may be extreme guilt and shame over having prioritized your	At this stage, you dispute the previously held irrational beliefs and replace them with more functional ones. To do this, ask yourself questions	If the previously held belief doesn't stand up to the scrutiny of the questions in the disputation stage, you can replace or refine those

event in the above example might be being reminded of the great couple you and your ex were.

irrational.

The irrational belief may be, "I should have stuck it out a little longer. I'm so selfish."

own wellness. This may even prompt you to go back to your abuser.

such as:

Is this belief supported by factual evidence?

Is there any evidence against this belief?

What is the worst and best possible outcome if I let go of this belief?

Rather than accepting the beliefs as the ultimate truth, you'll now analyze them. Take a look at this example disputation dialogue:

What's the evidence for and against the belief that I was selfish?

I gave this relationship

beliefs.

The effective new belief may be, "I'm not selfish. I have my personal boundaries and no one has the right to disrespect them."

everything I had. Sure, I expected some things in return, such as my partner's unconditional acceptance, support, and validation. But that's not selfish. The more I gave, the more my ex took. They were the selfish one.

What's the best and worst that could happen if I discard this belief?

There's no disadvantage to discarding this belief, but I may just be able to live more freely and without guilt if I stop calling myself selfish.

Although this disputation dialogue seems perfectly simple on paper, it may get tricky when you apply it in real life. That's why I say this is a journey best guided by an objective therapist to nudge you when you get stuck. But regardless of whether you do it on your own or with a therapist, remember that you won't reach the stage of having an effective new belief overnight. You've held those faulty beliefs for years, maybe even decades, and you need to allow yourself some time to discard them. So, don't be too harsh on yourself—this exercise may need to be repeated several times before you see positive results.

Dialectical Behavior Therapy

Now, let's move on to another form of behavior therapy that can work wonders with abuse survivors who also struggle with eating disorders, substance abuse, anxiety, and depression. The goal of dialectal behavior therapy (DBT) is to help you regulate the emotions that may have been deeply suppressed and dysregulated thanks to the abuser's temper tantrums and rage episodes. While there are many applications of this type of therapy, I want to highlight the mindfulness and emotional regulation skills that are especially important in our current context.

DBT is founded on the core principle that more than one thing can be true simultaneously. For instance, you can have a deep emotional concern for your abuser yet not want to be around them due to their abusive and manipulative patterns. The core of this therapeutic approach is to help you make peace with these contradicting notions without suppressing your emotions. Let's look at a couple of activities that abuse survivors find particularly helpful in emotional regulation and distress tolerance.

Mindfulness Meditation

DBT's focus on mindfulness encourages you to stay in the present moment and experience thoughts and emotions as they come rather than judging them. This may be easier said than done. Here are step-by-step instructions to get you started:

1. Sit in a quiet, distraction-free, and comfortable space.

2. Close your eyes and focus your attention on your breath. Also, pay attention to any other sensations you may experience in your body.

3. If your mind wanders to regrets of the past or worries about the future, gently bring it back to your breath in the present moment.

4. Practice doing this for 10–15 minutes at your preferred time of day.

As you do this every day, you may realize that your habit of living in the past or the future is completely destroying your ability to experience the present moment as it comes. Eventually, your mindfulness is likely to extend well beyond the act of meditation, allowing you to experience your emotions—and life at large—in a much fuller and more present manner.

The Ice Cube Technique

As mentioned earlier in our discussion of PTSD, survivors of narcissistic abuse may have experiences such as panic-inducing flashbacks and vivid nightmares regarding abuse episodes from the past. These can cause extreme overwhelm, completely hijacking their ability for rational thought. DBT prescribes several techniques for such circumstances, one of which is the ice cube technique. Anytime the individual feels overwhelmed with undesirable thoughts and emotions, they're urged to hold an ice cube in their hand. The intense (but harmless) sensation of cold becomes their anchor to the physical reality, distracting them from being carried away by the overwhelming emotions.

If an ice cube isn't immediately accessible, you can consider another version of this grounding activity known as the 5–4–3–2–1 technique. Here, you'll use all your senses (rather than just the sense of touch in the ice cube technique) to ground yourself in the present. The exercise involves identifying five objects you can see, four textures you can touch, three sounds you can hear, two aromas you can smell, and one flavor you can taste. These exercises allow you to step back from your emotions for a moment and view the situation as it is rather than how your mind imagines it to be.

Eye Movement Desensitization and Reprocessing

Eye movement desensitization and reprocessing (EMDR) is yet another extremely effective therapeutic module for survivor recovery. It's distinct from other therapies in that, while other therapies target the role of thoughts and emotions in the recovery process, EMDR focuses specifically on the memory of the abusive experiences. Therefore, this therapeutic intervention tends to be brief and doesn't require digging too deeply into the issues.

EMDR is based on the central principle that during any kind of trauma, the brain's memory storage becomes warped. Under normal circumstances, your brain is excellent at encoding events in ways that make their recall smooth. However, when there's trauma involved, it's almost as if there's a glitch in the system, leading to the faulty storage of memories as a result of them not being processed adequately. This can create significant hurdles in the healing process, as you may be faced with traumatic flashbacks and memories at the most unexpected times—and as a result of very subtle triggers, such as noises, smells, or even tastes.

Undergoing EMDR therapy requires you to access specific traumatic memories under guided instructions combined with eye movements and other forms of rhythmic left–right (bilateral) stimulation (e.g., tones or taps). This stimulation is effective in reducing the vividness and emotion of the unprocessed memory. EMDR therapy typically requires six to twelve sessions depending on the intensity of the trauma being tackled.

Rebuilding Self

As critical as therapeutic support is in your healing journey, your growth work between those sessions also makes a huge difference. It's important to recognize that leaving the abusive relationship may even feel worse in the beginning for two reasons. Firstly, you may well be experiencing post-separation abuse from the narcissist (possibly from a distance). Secondly, in addition to all of the emotional trauma, you're now required to deal with a thousand more logistical details as you're now out of the comfort of familiarity. In the midst of all this, it's easy to feel like you've completely lost your identity and that escaping the abuse is the defining principle of your life.

I remember a profound thank-you note from one of my clients; here's an excerpt:

> For decades, my husband chipped away at my joy, pride, and everything else that made me, *me*... until one fine day, I couldn't even recognize myself in the mirror. It was like a stranger was staring back at me, and that's the day I decided I couldn't stay any longer. I made the exit plan and I got out. And, yes, it felt empowering and liberating for the first couple of days. But as the novelty wore on, reality hit me like a ton of bricks. I had expected that leaving the abusive relationship would solve all my problems. Unfortunately, it didn't. I had to reclaim my identity if I were to feel like anything close to my old self. And that was no lesser feat than getting out of the narcissistic relationship. That was where the real adventure began.

This reclaiming of identity is a deeply personal and unique experience that everyone takes on at their own pace and in their own way. But no matter how unique this experience is, you must pay close attention to three critical facets of this growth—understanding the significance of therapy in your journey (which we've covered above), rebuilding your self by working on your own self-worth and self-talk, and creating a tool kit of daily strategies that you can keep handy.

Working on Self-Worth

The first step in raising your self-worth is recognizing the different ways in which you demean yourself. It's almost as if you've carried the critical, belittling voice of the abuser in your head. This is why you must assess your self-talk. We've already discussed how you can modify your negative self-talk. Now, let's see the different irrational patterns that may be eating away at your sense of self-worth and require modification. These irrational patterns are called cognitive distortions, and it's certainly helpful to be aware of them:

- **Discounting the positive:** After years of being with a narcissist, you may have been conditioned to downplay your accomplishments. Every time you're complimented, you may say something like, "Oh, that was nothing" instead of accepting the compliment with a "Thank you." I had a client who realized that every time someone complimented her cooking, she'd always give them a long-winded description of the recipe rather than just saying thank you. She became so uncomfortable with compliments that she felt compelled to distract the person complimenting her.

- **Personalizing:** This is especially common among abuse survivors as they keep blaming themselves for the undesirable turn that their relationship has taken: "I knew it would make my ex mad when I went no-contact, and now look what's happened!"

- **Filtering:** You may be so overwhelmed by the difficulties of leaving that you completely filter out the positives, which may force you to go back—or never leave in the first place.

- **Jumping to conclusions:** You may find yourself tangled in what people might say about you. For instance, you might engage in mind-reading, where you assume that people pity you and don't really care about helping you. You may also engage in fortune-telling, trying to predict the future (mostly in a negative light) after you leave: "I'll never be able to get out of this debt that my partner has pushed me into."

- **Magnification:** This is the tendency of abuse survivors to magnify their flaws and maybe even minimize the flaws of the abuser even after they leave. They may say something like, "I sometimes feel like our relationship would still be great if I hadn't pushed him for the wedding. We'd known each other for two years, but he kept saying he wasn't ready." Even after leaving, the survivor may not realize that the narcissist was merely future-faking and instead magnify the negative impact of their own gentle nudging.

- **Catastrophizing:** A narcissist may push their victim to be so codependent that they cannot imagine their life without the abusive relationship. The abuser has played into the victim's low self-esteem, so they believe the abuser when they tell them that they'll fail in life without them; this strengthens their bond with the abuser. This leaves them perpetually stuck between a rock and a hard place, neither of which they can envision escaping successfully.

- **Emotional reasoning:** Emotional abuse creates a climate of such insecurity that survivors often believe absolutely irrational thoughts despite heaps of evidence against them. Take, for instance, a girl who grows up *feeling* fat though her weight is perfectly within the healthy range. Unfortunately, this kind of emotional reasoning, which *the abuser encourages,* can continue long after the survivor leaves the narcissistic relationship behind, and it can keep eroding their confidence if left unchecked.

- **Shoulds and musts:** Emotional abuse can fill the survivor's head with unreasonable ideals, which may even be reinforced by the larger sociocultural context: "You must be the perfect partner/parent all the time." "You must put others' needs before your own." "You must be the best at what you do." If these conditions aren't met, the survivor feels that they might as well call themself a total failure. Examining your negative self-talk will likely yield several shoulds and musts that you chain yourself to. Being perfect isn't the goal; being healthy mentally, emotionally, and physically is.

Remember that this isn't an exhaustive list, but it contains the most common cognitive distortions I see in abuse survivors.

But what do you do once you've identified these flawed patterns of thinking? You'd use the therapeutic strategies listed in the previous section to replace these patterns with healthier ways of thinking that allow you to see the immense potential you hold within yourself.

A Strategic Tool Kit

Finally, here are a few tools that can facilitate the implementation of the principles discussed above and act as the perfect boosts for your self-worth:

- **Gratitude:** After having been repeatedly told some version of "You ought to be grateful to have me in your life" by your narcissistic abuser, it's hard to find things to be grateful for. But now that you're free from the abuser's clutches, it's time to redefine gratitude and practice it the way it's meant to be done. So many of my clients say they practice gratitude, but in reality, they're merely saying thank you or listing the things they ought to be grateful for. Here's the thing: Gratitude isn't about making a list; rather, it's about feeling the joy and hope that are often found in the little things life offers.

  I tell my clients to keep a "gratitude rock" in their pocket, which is just a normal rock that serves as a reminder to be thankful. Every time they touch it, they have to think of something they feel grateful for and truly experience the joy that comes with thinking about that thing. You don't always need a rock, though; you could express this gratitude by journaling about it. It could be a puppy you saw on the way to work, a flower blooming in all its glory, listening to a moving piece of music, or even watching a child play innocently and screeching with happiness. You may be waiting for big things to happen to be grateful, but once you allow these little joys to fill you up, you'll realize that those grand things are only a bonus.

- **Positive affirmations:** Much like gratitude, positive affirmations tend to take on an almost mechanical form when people try to turn them into daily practice. The truth is, positive affirmations are a beautiful way to tap into the abundance around you. Simple statements such as "I'm enough" or "I'm healing" can be incredibly empowering—if only you allow them to be, that is. Try closing your eyes and feeling the warmth of these statements spread across your chest and then your whole body. Visualize living your most fulfilling life as you repeat these statements to yourself. Feel the joy, peace, and contentment of that life as if it's happening to you in the present moment.

- **Social connections:** Many survivors feel so hurt and broken by their most treasured relationships that they simply withdraw. At the root of this behavior are multiple layers of shame and guilt for having "failed" at these relationships. As stated above, many or even most of these assumptions are in themselves faulty and don't stand the scrutiny of rational thought. Though it's absolutely natural to feel betrayed, it's important to realize that the only way of healing the trauma caused by abusive relationships is to foster healthy, reciprocal connections. These may be found in your social circle or in therapeutic settings such as support groups and forums, as mentioned previously.

- **Assertive boundary-setting:** If there's one thing you'll value more than anything else after abuse, it's your sense of personal boundaries. What you may not realize is that not only do these boundaries protect you, but they also propel your self-worth by creating a sense of agency. The feeling that you're in charge of your own life has a massive impact on your healing and recovery. It's important to remind yourself that your needs, feelings, and desires are separate from those of others, even those dear to you, and it's okay to say no when your boundaries aren't aligned.

Contrary to what some may believe, this assertive boundary-setting isn't necessarily a natural instinct. We, as humans, are always looking for connection, and it's easy to overlook the need for boundaries in this pursuit. The point is that assertive boundary-setting is a skill you must rehearse endlessly.

Remember that there are two key aspects to healthy boundaries: One is to gain clarity about your own needs, and the other is to effectively communicate those needs to others. Practice taking responsibility for the way you feel. That means no more discounting your own authority by saying things like, "*I don't know* but I feel like I need space," or "*I'm not sure* but maybe I need some more time." Own up to your needs and express them as confidently and concisely as possible. This is where your assertiveness practice will pay off. When you become comfortable with this assertiveness, you'll see that fulfilling, healthy, and meaningful relationships are waiting just around the corner.

- **Self-care:** The term self-care is so misused in the mainstream media that I frequently have to urge my clients to unlearn their ideas about it. Self-care is portrayed as an expensive indulgence (spa treatments and whatnot!) that only a few can afford. In reality, self-care has nothing to do with these consumerist constructs. What many people don't understand is that self-care isn't always about immediate gratification and pleasure. Sure, a spa day may feel great once in a while, but it doesn't serve the purpose of self-care in the long run. Therefore, it's important to remember that self-care is about recognizing your emotional and physical needs and making sure you nourish them as frequently as possible. This may include all of the practices discussed above, in addition to the many unique ones that bring you peace. Something as simple as sleeping in, all the way to something more spiritual such as praying, may all be forms of self-care that strengthen your sense of self and give you more confidence to keep moving forward.

Remember that all these strategies, positive as they may be, can feel overwhelming if you try to implement them all at once. So, start small and implement a habit that feels easier than the others to begin with. You can then incorporate more as you go along. As always, remember that the first step is the most crucial one, and things will get much easier if you power through the initial bumps.

Chapter 8:

Breaking the Cycle for Others

In the previous chapter, I mentioned a sense of agency in the context of boundary-setting. However, this sense of agency has a much broader implication in the recovery of trauma survivors. Many of these survivors find that the best way to heal their emotional wounds is by helping others break these abusive cycles in their own lives. Of course, even though giving back is immensely fulfilling, it's important to prioritize your own healing before you start taking on the responsibility of helping others. If and when you do decide to take this on, you might want to consider two aspects: addressing the intergenerational impact of abuse within your own family, and preventive strategies you can use as a bystander to help those who aren't necessarily connected to you.

Generational Healing

Intergenerational abuse is a cycle of trauma passed down across generations. For instance, you may have received this cursed inheritance when you were a child yourself, or you may unknowingly be passing it on to the next generation as the abusive relationship with your partner unfolds. Remember that there are two variations here— one where the abuser is abusive toward the child and one where the abuser intentionally manipulates the child to get back at you. Either way, children may bear the brunt of the abuser's tactics and be left with a host of behavioral, psychological, and emotional problems.

As discussed earlier, children who grow up in these abusive environments often grow up to be abusers themselves. This manifestation may be stronger when the child is exposed to certain toxic social standards about gender roles and entitlement. For example, imagine being told that it's okay to get things by force because that's the sign of a true man, or that you aren't allowed to cry or express your emotions because that's just a girly thing to do. You can imagine how this, combined with narcissism, can turn into a dangerous cocktail.

Therefore, you must make special efforts to break the cycle, especially if children are involved. Here are a few things you can do:

- **Offering stability:** Time and again, we've highlighted how you might need to maintain contact with the narcissist if you're co-parenting a child. As we've seen, this can get tremendously difficult, as the narcissist may often indulge in counter-parenting by letting the child do things you'd never allow, badmouthing you in front of them, and telling them that you're the reason why you aren't a family anymore—or even that you don't care about them. While you can't do much about what the abuser does, you sure can ensure you have a strong and stable relationship with your child. It's important that you stick to a consistent disciplining approach, regardless of what the narcissist says. This will ensure your child has the stability they deserve, minus the drama.

- **Recognizing abusive dynamics in pop culture:** This might sound old school, but the emergence of social media has resulted in a dramatic change in the conditioning around narcissism. It's almost as if we're promoting a narcissistic need for attention with all the likes and follows. Needless to say, the mainstream media has also not been immune to this. When we glorify manipulation and abuse as charming strengths, such as ambition and perseverance, we also run the risk of telling future generations that it's okay to be that way. Again, you may not be able to control the big picture of societal values, but whenever you encounter these themes, it's important to address them. Talk to your children about the consequences that these themes bring up for others. Your children may not understand the abusive dynamics in your relationship just yet, but having these conversations can help them make better sense of things as they grow older.

- **Promoting a culture of consent:** Many people may believe that lectures are what cement their kids' perceptions about consent. However, when you talk the talk, you also need to walk the walk. This demands that you encourage your children to set their own boundaries and also that you respect those boundaries. This doesn't mean you give in to all their demands. But it's important, nonetheless, to talk about these things. Talk to your children about different kinds of boundaries—physical, emotional, and sexual. Encourage them to explore how they feel when these boundaries are violated, then nudge them to extend the same empathetic perspective toward others' boundaries. Again, you can't expect a child to understand the complex nature of boundaries that even we adults seem to miss sometimes. That being said, it's critical for their own safety and the safety of others that they're introduced to the constructs of boundaries and consent from a young age.

Preventing Abuse as a Bystander

Intervening as a bystander can be especially tricky in circumstances with emotional abuse. Again, the general conditioning here may be, "Physical abuse is definitely unacceptable, but with emotional abuse, there may be some complex underlying conflict that you may not know of." It comes down to one question: Does any "underlying conflict" justify one individual (who's often more powerful than the other) aggressively ridiculing the other and stripping them of the basic human dignity that everyone deserves? The answer is a strong, resounding "no." Furthermore, these escalated situations can very well lead to physical aggression, which means that when such abuse unfolds in public places, it may be the bystanders' responsibility to put a stop to it.

This brings us to the next hurdle of *how*. Many bystanders who wish to help may just not know how to do so. They don't want to escalate the situation and bring harm to the victim. But they also know that turning around and walking away isn't the best response either. So, what do they do? Here are some tips that bystanders can follow to ensure they help the victim in the best possible manner, without endangering themselves:

- **Ask the victim directly:** First and foremost, you might want to speak directly to the victim, asking them if they're okay. You may even ask them something like, "Can I do something to help?" This can be a little more complicated than it looks, because the victim may feel too intimidated to ask for help. Therefore, if possible, try to get the victim away from the perpetrator when they answer. I remember a client whose ex started getting extremely verbally abusive at a pub, to the point where she feared he might get violent. The moment he left to get another drink, the women at the next table rushed over to see if she needed help, gathered a crowd to make sure the boyfriend couldn't get anywhere close to the victim, and didn't leave her side until the police got involved. My client recalled this as the moment when she realized she wasn't alone, even though she felt that way.

- **Create a distraction:** Let's say you're hosting a house party and your friend starts verbally abusing his girlfriend. Here, as the situation escalates, there's no way to get the victim away or talk to her, but you can still see that she's distressed and intimidated. The best thing to do here may be to distract the perpetrator. This doesn't mean becoming aggressive with them; that could blow the situation way out of control, endangering both your own and the victim's safety. Instead, try cutting off the conversation with something like, "How about some music?" and then leading the abuser to the dance floor while the victim gets some breathing space. It's essential that someone stays with the victim, too. Of course, these situations are extremely specific, so you might need to think on your feet to create safe distractions when faced with this kind of scenario.

- **Rally other bystanders:** Abusive situations are intimidating not only for the victims but also for the bystanders. Approaching these situations all on your own can be dangerous. Therefore, it's best to get more relevant people, such as friends of the victim and the perpetrator—or authority figures such as security guards, managers, or even police, if needed—to help defuse the situation appropriately.

- **Raise awareness about available resources:** This strategy is more of a post-abuse intervention. Once the victim has got over the immediate shock of an abusive episode, it's crucial that they're made aware of the available resources. Here are a few to keep in mind (Dateline NBC, 2021):

- o Call 911 in the event of immediate physical danger.

- o Safe Horizon can be reached on their 24/7 hotline at 1-800-621-HOPE (4673).

- o The National Domestic Violence Hotline can be reached at 1-800-799-SAFE (7233).

- o You can look up local resources in the online directory of the National Coalition Against Domestic Violence.

Remember that even as you take a proactive stance to help others break the cycle of abuse, you cannot take responsibility for their healing; they must do it on their own. All you can do is provide support to the best of your capabilities. Recovering from narcissistic abuse is a roller-coaster ride, and the only person you can be responsible for is yourself.

Conclusion

In 1967, Steven Maier and Martin Seligman (considered the father of positive psychology) conducted an intriguing experiment (Nickerson, 2024). They placed dogs in a specially created chamber that could deliver electric shocks. The dogs were divided into two groups: those who could escape the shocks by pressing a lever, and those who couldn't escape no matter what they did.

In the second phase, the chamber was slightly modified in that it was now divided into two parts—one that still delivered electric shocks and another that didn't. A small box separated these two sections, and the dog could easily jump over to escape the side that gave shocks. The researchers were stunned to see that only the dogs who'd previously learned to press the lever made any sort of attempt to escape the shocks. On the other hand, the dogs that believed there was no escape didn't even consider trying to find a way out. They simply sat on the electrified floor, trembling with what was termed "learned helplessness."

This learned helplessness has a huge role to play in abuse victims feeling stuck in their situations. I see this often in my practice, when an individual who's grown up experiencing traumatic interactions with their primary caregiver may simply give up and believe the same to be their fate, even in adulthood. If there's one thing you take from this book, then let it be this: You have the power to change your reality. It's all about learning the right responses to the abuser and building the courage to put yourself before others.

I'm not going to lie—it will be a tough climb. But I promise you, it will be worth every bit of effort you put in and more. No matter what your current situation is and no matter how cut off you feel from the world, I assure you that if you reach out, you'll find several hands reaching back. So, take your time, make your choice, and you'll find the most valuable gem you've ever owned somewhere along the way: yourself.

~~~~~

If you've found this book to be helpful, please leave a review. My mission is to reach out to as many victims of abuse as possible to make them realize this: Not only is it possible for them to survive abuse, but they can also *thrive*.

As for your journey, whatever you're doing, wherever this book meets you, please take good care of yourself. Be safe, use the mentioned resources, and reach out to trusted others. I hope you believe in your strength to fly as much as I do and make the leap of faith. All the best!

–Dr. Mel

References

ADR Times. (2024, February 5). *Emotional abuse in the workplace.* https://adrtimes.com/emotional-abuse-in-the-workplace

Alberta Children's Services. (n.d.). *Abuse in same-sex and LGBTQ* relationships..* https://www.humanservices.alberta.ca/documents/NCN1375-abuse-in-same-sex-LGBTQ-relationships-booklets.pdf

American Psychological Association. (n.d.). *Eye movement desensitization and reprocessing (EMDR) therapy.* https://www.apa.org/ptsd-guideline/treatments/eye-movement-reprocessing

The Beatles. (2018, June 17). *I'm looking through you (remastered 2009)* [Video]. YouTube. https://www.youtube.com/watch?v=gH6i9JAdJrQ

Brewster, M. P. (2000). Stalking by former intimates: Verbal threats and other predictors of physical violence. *Violence and Victims, 15*(1), 41–54. https://pubmed.ncbi.nlm.nih.gov/10972513/

Chan, K. (2023, September 26). *How narcissists use future faking to manipulate you into a relationship.* Verywell Mind. https://www.verywellmind.com/how-to-spot-future-faking-in-narcissistic-relationships-7968853

Clarke, J. (2023, December 5). *How to recognize a covert narcissist.* Verywell Mind. https://www.verywellmind.com/understanding-the-covert-narcissist-4584587

Cleveland Clinic. (n.d.-a). *Cortisol.* https://my.clevelandclinic.org/health/articles/22187-cortisol

Cleveland Clinic. (n.d.-b). *Elder abuse.*
https://my.clevelandclinic.org/health/articles/15583-elder-abuse

Cleveland Clinic. (n.d.-c). *PTSD (post-traumatic stress disorder.*
https://my.clevelandclinic.org/health/diseases/9545-post-traumatic-stress-disorder-ptsd

Cuncic, A. (2024, January 30). *How to spot a sense of entitlement in someone you know.* Verywell Mind.
https://www.verywellmind.com/what-is-a-sense-of-entitlement-5120616

Dateline NBC. (2021, March 12). *Emotional abuse resources.* NBC News.
https://www.nbcnews.com/dateline/emotional-abuse-resources-n1260929

DoctorRamani. (2020a, April 1). *What is "hoovering"? (Glossary of narcissistic relationships)* [Video]. YouTube.
https://www.youtube.com/watch?v=yPc7UxIfMfY

DoctorRamani. (2020b, May 14). *Everything you need to know about the 7 types of narcissists* [Video]. YouTube.
https://www.youtube.com/watch?v=4jfRGnG--H4&list=PL3QtnfcMTMhHGiFOlFrd1aid5AqzWxdgI&index=1

DoctorRamani. (2020c, May 20). *Malignant narcissists: Everything you need to know (Part 1/3)* [Video]. YouTube.
https://www.youtube.com/watch?v=3J4MEQ3N03w&list=PL3QtnfcMTMhHGiFOlFrd1aid5AqzWxdgI&index=7

DoctorRamani. (2022, September 16). *This is not how narcissists gray rock* [Video]. YouTube.
https://www.youtube.com/watch?v=rkJsl_mnRe4

DoctorRamani. (2023a, January 4). *What makes a narcissist become a psychopath?* [Video]. YouTube.
https://www.youtube.com/watch?v=XtzNHBtph-o

DoctorRamani. (2023b, October 16). *Red flags to watch out for before you get too serious with a narcissist* [Video]. YouTube. https://www.youtube.com/watch?v=c0Zh8DzibXg

DoctorRamani. (2023c, January 29). *Watch this! To learn how to break the trauma bond with a narcissist* [Video]. YouTube. https://www.youtube.com/watch?v=vIFJHH8V8go

DoctorRamani. (2024, March 29). *Different ways of leaving a narcissistic relationship* [Video]. YouTube. https://www.youtube.com/watch?v=bQkCfbuTTzg

Dorwart, L. (2024, October 31). *5 types of narcissism and core signs*. Verywell Health. https://www.verywellhealth.com/narcissistic-personality-disorder-types-5213256

Durvasula, R. (2024). *It's not you*. Penguin.

Dye, H. L. (2019). Is emotional abuse as harmful as physical and/or sexual abuse? *Journal of Child & Adolescent Trauma, 13*(4), 399–407. https://doi.org/10.1007/s40653-019-00292-y

Domestic Violence Center of Chester County. (n.d.). *Fast facts & statistics*. https://dvcccpa.org/fast-facts-statistics

Ferguson, S. (2023, August 8). *11 common post-separation abuse tactics*. Healthline. https://www.healthline.com/health/post-separation-abuse

Financial abuse: Spotting the signs and leaving safely. (n.d.). Money Helper. https://www.moneyhelper.org.uk/en/family-and-care/talk-money/financial-abuse-spotting-the-signs-and-leaving-safely

Fishman, S. (2024a, May 5). *Spotting and dealing with a smear campaign by a narcissist*. Psych Central. https://psychcentral.com/disorders/ways-narcissists-smear-others

Fishman, S. (2024b, May 16). *What does it look like when a narcissist apologizes?* Psych Central.

https://psychcentral.com/disorders/when-a-narcissist-makes-an-apology

Fleming, V. (Director). (1939). *The Wizard of Oz* [Film]. Metro-Goldwyn-Mayer (MGM).

Fry, R., Aragão, C., Hurst, K., & Parker, K. (2023, April 13). *In a growing share of U.S. marriages, husbands and wives earn about the same*. Pew Research Center. https://www.pewresearch.org/social-trends/2023/04/13/in-a-growing-share-of-u-s-marriages-husbands-and-wives-earn-about-the-same

Gordon, S. (2023, August 30). *How to leave an abusive relationship safely*. Verywell Mind. https://www.verywellmind.com/making-a-safety-plan-to-escape-abusive-relationship-5069959

Green, J. M. (n.d.). *A quote by John Mark Green*. Goodreads. https://www.goodreads.com/quotes/7389719-toxic-people-attach-themselves-like-cinder-blocks-tied-to-your

Gupta, S. (2024, May 15). *How to identify and escape a narcissistic abuse cycle*. Verywell Mind. https://www.verywellmind.com/narcissistic-abuse-cycle-stages-impact-and-coping-6363187

Heim, C. M., Mayberg, H. S., Mletzko, T., Nemeroff, C. B., & Pruessner, J. C. (2013). Decreased cortical representation of genital somatosensory field after childhood sexual abuse. *The American Journal of Psychiatry*, *170*(6), 616–623. https://doi.org/10.1176/appi.ajp.2013.12070950

History Today. (2018, July 7). *The myth of Narcissus*. https://www.historytoday.com/archive/foundations/myth-narcissus

Holmes, L. (2024, March 10). *How emotional abuse in childhood changes the brain*. Verywell Mind. https://www.verywellmind.com/childhood-abuse-changes-the-brain-2330401

Huecker, M. R., King, K. C., Jordan, G. A., & Smock, W. (2023). *Domestic violence.* StatPearls Publishing. https://www.ncbi.nlm.nih.gov/books/NBK499891

Implementing yellow rock communication when co-parenting with a narcissist. (n.d.). One Mom's Battle. https://www.onemomsbattle.com/blog/implementing-yellow-rock-communication-when-co-parenting-with-a-narcissist

Jonason, P. K., & Krause, L. (2013). The emotional deficits associated with the dark triad traits: Cognitive empathy, affective empathy, and alexithymia. *Personality and Individual Differences, 55*(5), 532–537. https://doi.org/10.1016/j.paid.2013.04.027

Kansas Legal Services. (2024, January 5). *Creating a safety plan.* https://www.kansaslegalservices.org/node/2643/creating-safety-plan

Karakurt, G., & Silver, K. E. (2013). Emotional abuse in intimate relationships: The role of gender and age. *Violence and Victims, 28*(5), 804–821. https://pmc.ncbi.nlm.nih.gov/articles/PMC3876290/#R27

Kassel, G. (2023, December 7). *9 signs you're dating a narcissist — and how to get out.* Healthline. https://www.healthline.com/health/mental-health/am-i-dating-a-narcissist

Kippert, A. (2019, January 30). *Stages of recovery after trauma.* DomesticShelters.org. https://www.domesticshelters.org/articles/after-abuse/stages-of-recovery-after-trauma

Kumari, V. (2020). Emotional abuse and neglect: time to focus on prevention and mental health consequences. *The British Journal of Psychiatry, 217*(5), 597–599. https://doi.org/10.1192/bjp.2020.154

Laderer, A. (2023, October 18). *Wait, can you get PTSD from narcissistic abuse?* Charlie Health.

https://www.charliehealth.com/post/ptsd-from-narcissistic-abuse

Larsen, L. S. (2024, September 29). *What are the 3 stages of trauma recovery?* Psychological Services of Lisa S. Larsen, PsyD. https://www.lisaslarsen.com/post/what-are-the-three-stages-of-trauma-recovery

Leder, S. (2021, July 1). *Let's get experimental: Cognitive dissonance.* Mayim Balik's Breakdown. https://www.bialikbreakdown.com/articles/lets-get-experimental-cognitive-dissonance

Liu, J., Deng, J., Zhang, H., & Tang, X. (2023). The relationship between child maltreatment and social anxiety: A meta-analysis. *Journal of Affective Disorders, 329,* 157–167. https://doi.org/10.1016/j.jad.2023.02.081

McLeod, S. (2023, October 29). *Schachter-Singer two-factor theory of emotion.* Simply Psychology. https://www.simplypsychology.org/schachter-singer-theory.html

Merriam-Webster. (n.d.). *Gaslight.* (n.d.). In *Merriam-Webster.com dictionary.* Retrieved December 10, 2024. https://www.merriam-webster.com/dictionary/gaslight

Nickerson, C. (2024, May 2). *Learned helplessness.* Simply Psychology. https://www.simplypsychology.org/learned-helplessness.html

Nunez, K. (2020, April 17). *What is the ABC model in cognitive behavioral therapy?* Healthline. https://www.healthline.com/health/abc-model

Pau, S. (2024, June 11). *Dr Ramani: How to cope in a relationship with a narcissist! #149 A millennial mind podcast* [Video]. YouTube. https://www.youtube.com/watch?v=UvdnAHE5VUA

Polinski, K. J., Bemis, E. A., Feser, M., Seifert, J., Demoruelle, M. K., Striebich, C. C., Brake, S., O'Dell, J. R., Mikuls, T. R., Weisman, M. H., Gregersen, P. K., Keating, R. M., Buckner, J., Nicassio,

P., Holers, V. M., Deane, K. D., & Norris, J. M. (2019). Perceived stress and inflammatory arthritis: A prospective investigation in the Studies of the Etiologies of Rheumatoid Arthritis (SERA) cohort. *Arthritis Care & Research, 72*(12), 1766–1771. https://doi.org/10.1002/acr.24085

Radell, M. L., Abo Hamza, E. G., Daghustani, W. H., Perveen, A., & Moustafa, A. A. (2021). The impact of different types of abuse on depression. *Depression Research and Treatment, 2021*(6654503), 1–12. https://doi.org/10.1155/2021/6654503

Rai, T., Mainali, P., Raza, A., Rashid, J., & Rutkofsky, I. (2019). Exploring the link between emotional child abuse and anorexia nervosa: A psychopathological correlation. *Cureus, 11*(8), e5318. https://doi.org/10.7759/cureus.5318

Rape, Abuse & Incest National Network. (n.d.). *Practicing active bystander intervention.* https://rainn.org/articles/practicing-active-bystander-intervention

Ritter, K., & Olsen, J. M. (2023, August 25). *What is Stockholm syndrome? It all started with a bank robbery 50 years ago.* AP News. https://apnews.com/article/stockholm-syndrome-history-origin-023ddcd3a14ac00a0ba88feb838574b3

Robinson, P., Wade, T., Herpertz-Dahlmann, B., Fernandez-Aranda, F., Treasure, J., & Wonderlich, S. (Eds.). (2024). *Eating disorders.* Springer.

Royse, D. D. (2016). *Emotional abuse of children.* Routledge.

Shah, N. (2025, February 4). *Powerful ABCDE model from REBT – complete guide with examples.* Institute of Clinical Hypnosis and Related Sciences. https://instituteofclinicalhypnosis.com/psychotherapy-coaching/abcde-model-rebt

Shahri, F., Zabihzadeh, A., Taqipanahi, A., Erfani Haromi, M., Rasouli, M., Saeidi Nik, A., & Eddy, C. M. (2024). I understand your pain but I do not feel it: Lower affective empathy in response to others' social pain in narcissism. *Frontiers in Psychology, 15.* https://doi.org/10.3389/fpsyg.2024.1350133

Shaw, G. B. (n.d.). *A quote by George Bernard Shaw.* Goodreads. https://www.goodreads.com/quotes/43033-never-wrestle-with-pigs-you-both-get-dirty-and-the

Smith, M., & Segal, J. (n.d.). *How to get out of an abusive relationship.* HelpGuide.org. https://www.helpguide.org/relationships/domestic-abuse/getting-out-of-an-abusive-relationship

Stray, S. M. (2019, July 24). *More relationships, more red flags: Identifying emotional abuse in polyamory.* Medium. https://medium.com/@loveinthesuburbs/more-relationships-more-red-flags-identifying-narcissistic-emotional-abuse-in-polyamory-48a1e95509ce

TalktoAngel. (2024, November 15). *Understanding Stockholm syndrome in romantic relationships.* https://www.talktoangel.com/blog/understanding-stockholm-syndrome-in-romantic-relationships

Testa & Pagnanelli, LLC. (2024, February 5). *How to prove my partner's narcissism ended my marriage.* https://www.tpfamilylaw.com/blog/2024/february/how-to-prove-my-partners-narcissism-ended-my-mar/

Tete, S. (2025, January 28). *What does a narcissist do at the end of a relationship?* Stylecraze. https://www.stylecraze.com/articles/what-a-narcissist-does-at-the-end-of-a-relationship

Thompson, J. (n.d.). *What is Stockholm syndrome?* WebMD. https://www.webmd.com/mental-health/what-is-stockholm-syndrome

Tian, L., Zhou, Z., & Huebner, E. S. (2023). Association between emotional abuse and depressive symptoms in Chinese children: The mediating role of emotion regulation. *Child Abuse &*

Neglect,   *139,*   106135. https://doi.org/10.1016/j.chiabu.2023.106135

Travers, M. (2024, June 19). *2 ways narcissists weaponize empathy for personal gain—by   a   psychologist.*   Forbes. https://www.forbes.com/sites/traversmark/2024/06/19/2-ways-narcissists-weaponize-empathy-for-personal-gain-by-a-psychologist/

Turner, I. N., Foster, J. D., & Webster, G. D. (2019). The dark triad's inverse relations with cognitive and emotional empathy: High-powered tests with multiple measures. *Personality and Individual Differences,*   *139,*   1–6. https://doi.org/10.1016/j.paid.2018.10.030

Vevers, S. (2023, August 29). *Early signs of abusive behavior.* Medical News Today.   https://www.medicalnewstoday.com/articles/early-signs-of-an-abusive-man

Vinney, C. (2024, May 10). *Projection as a defense mechanism.* Verywell Mind.   https://www.verywellmind.com/what-is-a-projection-defense-mechanism-5194898